The Disruption Dilemma

The Disruption Dilemma

Joshua Gans

The MIT Press
Cambridge, Massachusetts
London, England

This book was set in Sabon LT Std by Toppan Best-set Premedia Limited. Printed and bound in the United States of America.

Library of Congress Cataloging-in-Publication Data

Names: Gans, Joshua, 1968– author.
Title: The disruption dilemma / Joshua Gans.
Description: Cambridge, MA : The MIT Press, 2016. | Includes bibliographical references and index.
Identifiers: LCCN 2015039869 | ISBN 9780262034487 (hardcover : alk. paper)
Subjects: LCSH: Crisis management. | Organizational change.
Classification: LCC HD49 .G36 2016 | DDC 658.4/056—dc23 LC record available at
   http://lccn.loc.gov/2015039869

10   9   8   7   6   5   4   3   2   1

Contents

Preface

The word disruption was brought prominently to managerial attention by Clayton Christensen in his 1997 book *The Innovator's Dilemma*.[1] Since then, many business leaders have gone from being complacent about innovation and technical change as forces to being petrified by them. For Christensen's message was simple: just managing well does not make you safe. Indeed, it could be your downfall.

As a professor who keenly followed these developments daily, I wondered whether that initial message, for all the good that it did in shaking CEOs of big firms out of their comfort zones, had become lost in a mess of confusion that had many seeing disruption everywhere and using it to justify managerial decisions that were risky and not, ultimately, in their interests. In other words, had the pendulum swung too far? It is great to challenge your beliefs, but that doesn't necessarily mean you should hold none.

The original notion of disruption aimed to describe why great firms can fail. Today, use of the term has gotten out of control. Everything and everyone can supposedly be disruptive. Moreover, everyone is supposed to become disruptive. Though widely believed, none of these notions are obvious or obviously true. It is time to refocus the term exclusively on its initial use.

Writing this book began in angst as I watched these developments. Aside from Christensen, management academics have not geared their research to this area in proportion to the business interest in it. Why is that so? After all, disruption had hardly gone unnoticed by my colleagues or myself. We were certainly under no illusion that disruption meant something greater than what it actually was … right? But for some reason, academics had generally picked and chosen what they liked from Christensen's account.[2] We had not criticized his argument, because very few of us had taken the time to go beyond the headlines and delve deeply into his work. Moreover, we saw that many of his ideas actually had antecedents that we had known about long before Christensen hit the popular circuit, so we didn't engage with them as vigorously as we might have if he were the first person making these claims.

A relatively uncritical view of disruption in my teaching served a simple purpose; the notion resonated and had a kind of counterintuitive appeal. Who doesn't like the idea that successful companies end up being exposed precisely because they do the "right" thing? Who doesn't like the cautionary tale in which a new technology comes along, the market leader does all the right things (e.g., asks its customers if they want the new technology, and hears them when they say no), and the leader misses the boat? We want our students to be wary about conventional strategy and tools, and by golly, disruption made them wary.

Indeed, it made them and others fearful. Christensen's book really took off in 1999 when *Forbes* wrote[3] about how he had persuaded Intel's Andy Grove that Intel needed to explore lower-power chips for laptops.[4] Grove described the idea as "scary," and those words were subsequently emblazoned on the cover of Christensen's book. I'm not a historian of ideas, but it is tempting to theorize that following the dot-com bust and 9/11, the world's managers were receptive to a message of fear.

Print news media and higher education were facing radical changes to their business models in the name of disruption. Those who had been influenced by Christensen rose to his defense, reminding us that Steve Jobs, despite his well-known disdain for reading, had read Christensen's book. Marc Andreessen (Netscape's founder) seethed at the notion that disruption was a bad thing, placing it as a guiding principle. "To be AGAINST disruption is to be AGAINST consumer choice, AGAINST more people being served, and AGAINST shrinking inequality," he tweeted. "[T]he more Christensen-style disruption, and the faster, the better!"[5] A debate raged but did not really reach resolution.

All this convinced me that the time had come to sort the matter out, and my angst turned to the earnestness that led me to write this book. We needed to add back the other voices in academia and elsewhere to our understanding of the phenomenon of disruption. As a concept, disruption has become so pervasive that it is at risk of becoming useless.[6] This book's purpose is to take back the idea of disruption and refocus it on Christensen's original question: How is it that great companies, doing what made them great, can find themselves in trouble? And how can we advise them on what to do about their troubles? Many voices have had answers to those questions, and after two decades of chaotic evolution, it is time to bring them together.

This book is designed to help managers understand disruption and what to do about it. It will provide the tools, not just Christensen's but those of many others, that provide a complete picture of where disruption can come from and how it can be managed. And that is the message of this book: The evidence brought to bear is that disruption can be managed but that simple prescriptions—such as the mantra of self-disruption with its recommendation to disrupt your own business before others do—are rarely of use. Instead, tried-and-true methods of product development from the pre-Christensen era still find a place in a disruptive world. Here the chaos and confusion will be stripped away, and managers will be given the opportunity to refocus and take some control of the future destiny of their businesses. My desire is to turn rampant fear into cautious hope. This is not a book meant to bury disruption but instead to resurrect it and preserve its canonical status.

I would like to acknowledge the many conversations I have had over the course of many years that were relevant to this book. I am particularly in debt to Ajay Agrawal, Pierre Azoulay, Shane Greenstein, Rebecca Henderson, David Hsu, Roger Martin, Matt Marx, and Scott Stern who have developed my thinking in this area, and also to Clay Christensen who provided me with influential thoughts on the final manuscript. A special thanks to Tim Sullivan, David Champion, and my agent, Ted Weinstein, who pushed me to think carefully about how to express these ideas to a practical management audience. I thank several anonymous reviewers for encouraging me to make the book bolder and more direct in its message. I have benefited enormously from the insights and suggestions of my editor, Emily Taber. And finally I want to thank Jane Wu for her tireless research assistance and reviewing of countless drafts of what you will read here.

1

Introduction

At the dawn of Microsoft's Windows 1.0 in 1985, CEO Bill Gates saw an opportunity for a digital encyclopedia. It would be placed on a new medium, the CD-ROM, and could potentially be seen as a "must have" application, just like MS Word which was taking off on Apple's personal computers. A Microsoft executive, Min Yee, was charged with obtaining high-quality content for the new product and immediately turned up at the offices of Encyclopaedia Britannica, the company unambiguously at the top of the encyclopedia market. Perhaps Yee had not been schooled in the finer points of getting one's foot in the door, but he was quickly rebuffed by the Britannica team. Had he had the opportunity, Yee might have been able to explain that their turning him away would end up hurting Britannica more than Microsoft. Britannica's management, however, appeared to see only the cost of Microsoft's proposal to its legacy brand and not the upside.

That brand had been built by strong selling skills. The job for salespeople was to go door to door and sell families, usually middle-class ones, on spending $500 to $2,000 on an encyclopedia when no other book they owned was worth more than $100. As Microsoft noted, "no other broad-appeal content product in any category in any medium has a well-established single-user price point anywhere close to this."[1] But sell they did, in the hundred of thousands of sets each year. And why not? They were the best in breed with half a million entries all written by experts in their fields, including over one hundred Nobel laureates.

The sales pitch was not about selling books; it was literally about "selling dreams." Recounting his experience as a Britannica salesman just out of college in the 1970s, Josh Goldstein realized that he was not selling the text on the page but the promise of something more. If he selected the right household, he could pitch access to the best world's knowledge and with it a bright future for the family's children. Sometimes a customer chose the luxury-bound, premium set even without a hard sell from Goldstein:

Guilt stricken, I begged her to reconsider and go for the stripped down economy package since, as I assured her, the words on the pages were identical and would cost her $500.00 less. But she was adamant and signed the contract.[2]

For a few customers, the encyclopedia seller came to mean something more. Here is Michael Milton:

Yet it was this man, this anonymous figure, who sold, that is artfully (and I say, "gratefully") *persuaded*, my Aunt Eva to sign her name on a three-year plan that would promise to transport a poor, poverty-stricken Southern child from a five-acre farm, a hardscrabble farm at that, to tour the world without ever leaving his bedroom. There was never a greater encyclopedia then [sic] the Encyclopedia Britannica and never a greater voyage to be had.[3]

Decades later, Milton remembered the sales technique, the presentation of a couple of volumes the salesman carried with him, the full-color pictures, and the pitch that "to acquire the *Encyclopedia Britannica* was not merely a purchase, but an investment in the education of her boy." His Aunt Eva bought them for him and Milton devoured them accordingly.

As it turned out, while he may not have been alone, Milton was a rarity. Despite this sales pitch, even Britannica knew that the volumes were mainly for display. To own them and place them on shelves in a living room was a statement that the household cared about the education of their children. There, these symbols gathered dust, opened on average just one or two times a year.[4]

With that in mind, it is perhaps appropriate that I open this book with *Encyclopaedia Britannica* as an example of *disruption*: of how successful companies, continuing to do what made them successful, end up falling to the point of failure. The story of *Encyclopaedia Britannica* seems a simple one. After turning Microsoft away in 1985, it kept doing what it had done for decades. Meanwhile Microsoft acquired the content it needed from *Funk & Wagnalls* (ironically remembered as a poor person's *Britannica*) and launched *Encarta* which would sell millions of CDs, dwarfing *Britannica*'s best years. After its success, of course, *Encarta* followed a similar fate in its turn, falling by the wayside with the unexpected success of Wikipedia, an encyclopedia that wasn't a business at all. *Encyclopaedia Britannica*, now a shadow of its former self, opted to discontinue the print version and with it the encyclopedia salesperson in 2012.[5]

Anecdotes, however, are not all they might seem. Even the simplest accounts look very different when you brush away the dust and explore what really happened. First of all, for Britannica management, rejecting Microsoft was actually an easy decision. In 1985, Microsoft was still a young start-up, far from commanding the reputation it would a decade later. Computers themselves were in very few households (around 8.2 percent).[6] Finally, you could hardly display a CD-ROM in your home the way you could a shelf of encyclopedias. There was no symbolic display of the fact that your cared for your children's future, and thus, one could imagine, no incentive to make the purchase.

Given its management's information and perspective, then, Britannica was essentially right to dismiss Microsoft's proposal. Britannica was what we would today call a platform, and the main people it had to recruit, other than customers, were salespeople and contributors. While many today mock Wikipedia editors for doing their work for free, that was essentially the same deal for Britannica's expert contributors. They were paid little except for the prestige of having an entry on their resume. It is far from clear that these experts would feel the same way about contributing to a digital edition. More importantly, a lower-priced CD would not fit in with Britannica's sales process. Salespeople got paid on commission but in return needed to know that the company had their back. If Britannica started selling a digital computer product in stores, it could easily disrupt a careful balance of incentives and trust the firm had been built on. Indeed, even with the rejection of Microsoft, Britannica sales continued to grow in the years following—that is, until they peaked in 1990.

As early as 1983, salespeople were taught to dismiss digital options, claiming that it would take 100–200 floppy disks to hold just Britannica's index, that mainframe remote access would be clunky, that there wouldn't be enough words on a screen, and how could you search for an entry anyway? In fact, however, by the late 1980s Britannica was actively experimenting with digital media. It launched a "NewMedia" version of *Compton's Encyclopedia* in 1989 (with sound bites narrated by Patrick Stewart, of all people), becoming the first encyclopedia on CD-ROM. This was seen by *Business Week* as pathbreaking but it was also expensive, priced at $895.[7] Thus it failed to get any traction, and Britannica exited that line in 1993 with a sale of its NewMedia unit to the *Chicago Tribune*.

The early 1990s brought more experimentation from Britannica, though this was concentrated in its Advanced Technology Group based in La Jolla, California—half a continent away from the Chicago head office. They registered *EB.com* in 1993 before browsers existed, but when the browser arrived Britannica Online became available in 1994. This was not a sign of complacency about digitization but, in fact, a remarkably prescient assessment of the future.

So what happened? Britannica's sales peaked in 1990—three years before Microsoft launched *Encarta* at a price point of under $100. Britannica responded with its own CD-ROM, this time of its famous encyclopedia, but it sold for $1,200 (though the price steadily fell to $200 by 1996).[8] Britannica's digital offerings were actually successful but did little to stem the overall losses from the new intensity of competition.

In reality, *Encyclopaedia Britannica* was not competing with *Encarta* but instead with the computer.[9] Recall the sales pitch that Britannica was an educational offering and a way for parents to put their children on a new path. The path was valued at around $1,000, but during the 1990s, for a little bit more, you could buy a computer to fulfill the same dream, and with a relatively cheap encyclopedia included, thanks to Microsoft. Later on, with the Internet, you did not even need the Encarta add-on. While Britannica's salespeople may have been able to explain why their encyclopedia was the best *encyclopedia*, it is far from clear that they would have been in a position to take on the computer.

With the benefit of hindsight, was there something Britannica could have done to forestall disruption? As I have already noted, Britannica did, in fact, see change coming and set up a separate, independent division to deal with that change. The problem was that the division was ahead of its time. It did not generate a solution; instead, the solution would likely have had to involve Britannica investing simultaneously in different ways of delivering the dream of education. Imagine, for instance, an *Encyclopaedia Britannica*-branded computer around 1990, with the encyclopedia preinstalled. The dream could sit on a desk rather than a shelf. Now imagine how a door-to-door salesperson would have had to sell that dream. No longer could it be done with books under an arm; instead the salesperson would have to tote around a heavy computer and small monitor (there were no portables then) and then seamlessly set the thing up in people's homes. Add to that a complete retraining of the salesforce and it is hardly surprising that this option was never exercised.

Britannica's case illustrates all of the elements of disruption. It shows that good and farsighted managers might reasonably choose to minimize opportunities to catch a new technological wave. It also shows that even if they were to choose to try to catch it, the problem of coordinating the necessary organizational change would surely be a challenging one. It might well strike fear into the hearts of business leaders and suggest that perhaps there is only so much they could do.

Britannica demonstrates alternative mechanisms by which disruption can emerge and how it can be managed. On the consumer side, it looks like the digital products competing with *Encyclopaedia Britannica* were initially of lower quality, but ended up challenging it competitively later on. Britannica had experimented with digital products and had the means of riding the storm had it so chosen, but was unable to respond in the educational dreams market that it had traditionally dominated. To sell a dream in a digital form would have required Britannica to make a change in its organization; in other words, to become a completely different company. Indeed, it is arguable that no firm replaced Britannica in the dreams department; it was instead computers and the Internet that allowed families to put it together in another way.

Boxes of Disruption

While *Encyclopaedia Britannica* presents an example of a successful company losing its primary business due to a disruptive event, some companies have seen potential disruption coming from new entrants and taken action to avoid the consequences. An example of this is the Matson Navigation Company, which began in 1882 with sail-powered ships taking sugar between Hawaii and the mainland. It became the leading freight and passenger shipping company on that route by the early 1900s, having survived the conversion to steam.[10] More instructive for our purposes is how Matson dealt with and survived containerization.

Containerization was a revolution. Prior to 1956, freight was shipped using methods that dated back to the Phoenicians. Freight was loaded in a labor-intensive manner into the holds of ships at the departure port, and then taken out again at the destination port. Ship time in port was long, cargo had to be reloaded on land transport to get to customers, and labor costs had been steadily rising. Containerization changed all that, but the change was extensive: it wasn't just a matter of using a box. Ships had to be redesigned so that containers could sit on top rather than down below for easy loading and unloading. Ports needed to be redesigned with large cranes to handle container traffic and load containers onto truck and rail transport. Finally, the entire logistics, information flow, and contracting space had to be reengineered.[11]

This is the sort of change that requires companies to wipe the slate clean and start over. For that reason, it is often brought about by new entrants rather than established firms. And so it was with containerization. Malcolm McLean, a US trucking magnate, boldly sold his business and moved into container shipping in the 1950s.[12] He demonstrated what needed to be done by loading 58 container bodies of trucks onboard a modified tanker, the *Ideal-X*, and sailing it from Newark to Houston in April 1956. It took years of struggle, investment, union setbacks, port negotiations, government backing in the Vietnam War, and a standards war, but by the 1970s containerization had taken hold and McLean had come out on top with a global shipping empire.

Lost in the heroic entrepreneurial account were the activities of Matson. As documented by economic historian Marc Levinson in the early 1950s, Matson moved from being a sleepy Hawaiian conglomerate into a serious, logistics-minded shipping company. In the process Matson also started to engage in research and development to improve its operations. Whereas McLean fit the mold of what today would be called a start-up (moving quickly, launching minimum viable products, and aggressively acquiring customers), Matson's research proceeded slowly and carefully. The company's focus was on how to use new technology and approaches to optimize. It did not want to prove containerization could work; it wanted to find the best system that reduced total customer shipping costs.

Matson's research director, Foster Weldon, paid close attention to how the company's operations would benefit from containerization. Thus, when he observed that more cargo was shipped to Hawaii than from it, he knew that the savings had to play out taking into account the potential shipping of empty containers back to the mainland. For this reason, Matson, like many established firms, began with a hybrid system of ships with goods below and above deck. Moreover, by taking its time, it avoided some missteps that had plagued McLean. For instance, it saw the opportunity to build port-side cranes rather than ship-side ones for more efficient loading and unloading. This was especially important since its routes were almost exclusively between larger ports. The cranes themselves were specifically designed and built for the new system. Finally, to make it all work, Weldon's research department used computers to run the first-ever simulations to determine logistics, using data to determine optimal routes.

What Matson had done was to integrate its research operations into its main operations and, at the same time, to explore and experiment with multiple new technologies that it could use to improve its existing services. Later, when containerization was competing against traditional shipping companies on price and performance, Matson already had in place a system to hold its own and develop the Pacific routes. It bears emphasis that Matson lagged behind others in adopting the new technology, but when it did so, it was able to benefit from learning and to choose a system optimized for its customers.

Dilemmas: Old and New

Britannica and Matson were both successful firms that faced disruption in the form of a new technology. In both cases, the industry was completely transformed by that new technology. However, while Britannica became a disrupted firm, Matson sailed on. Unpacking why their fates were so different is the purpose of this book.

While it is hard to compare encyclopedias and ocean shipping, there are similarities in the Britannica and Matson cases. As already noted, each faced a new technology that transformed their respective industries. Importantly, the senior management in both firms realized the potential of the new technology and sought early on, well ahead of most in the market, to enact strategies to respond to it. However, Britannica and Matson took distinct approaches in implementing that response. Understanding those different choices and their implications is the key to seeing how to deal with disruption.

Britannica and Matson faced variants of what has become known as "the innovator's dilemma." While the term was coined and explored by Clayton Christensen in his famous 1997 book of that title, the dilemmas have been posed in various forms through the academic literature on management both prior to Christensen and also contemporaneously with him. The dilemma an established firm faces when dealing with disruption—usually in the form of a new technology or innovation—is that seemingly good management practices not only can fail to deal with disruption but can, in fact, be a hindrance in finding a way of dealing with it. When Britannica explored digital technologies in the mid to late 1980s, its main encyclopedia business was thriving, and accommodating a digital product would require reengineering the entire organization. As a consequence, its approach was to wall off its digital endeavors, allowing them to be pursued freely in an autonomous unit. Matson faced the same organizational issues in adopting containerization for its shipping fleet, but rather than creating a separate unit to pursue this, from the start it adopted a new organizational structure that tightly integrated research and commercial divisions. Thus, it exposed the entire organization to change and in the process faced a slower path to adopting containerization.

The difference between dealing with disruption via a walled-off, independent unit and doing so with a more tightly integrated organizational structure is at the center of this book. To be sure, the independence path has received the most attention in recent times, due to its advocacy by Clayton Christensen under the mandate of disrupting one's own company before a competitor does. However, the integration path stemmed from a distinct approach to analyzing disruption that emerged at the same time as Christensen's. This approach was put forward mainly by Rebecca Henderson. Both Christensen and Henderson were Harvard PhD students around 1990, both looked at what we now call disruption as part of their seminal thesis work, and today both are professors at Harvard Business School. How they came to such distinct viewpoints will be covered later in this book.

To anticipate where this journey will take us, we will see that independence as a means of dealing with disruption has some inherent flaws that undermine its effectiveness. This is both theoretically the case—as every independent unit eventually needs to be integrated into the mainline organization, creating the very conflicts it was set up to avoid—but is also true as part of the historical record—very few firms have used independent units to successfully avoid disruption.

The track record on dealing with disruption via an integrated organizational structure is, in my opinion, stronger but itself leads to a new dilemma. To stave off disruption, integration comes with a price. Organizations that have integrated ways of dealing with radical technological change tend to be slower-moving and also tend, at any given point in time, not to operate at their most efficient. Consequently, while they tend to be long-lived and shielded when there are multiple disruptive waves, they tend not to lead or dominate their markets. Thus, a core dilemma firms must grapple with is whether to integrate for sustainability or adopt alternative structures to gain more transient but profitable market positions.

A Full Picture

Let me now map the journey that will lead us to this core dilemma about disruption and how to deal with it. Disruption, as a word, has been oversimplified and overapplied; there has been a tendency to see it without any shades of gray. For instance, the initial interest of Clayton Christensen's approach was that well-managed companies could fail precisely because they were well managed. But since then "disruption" has entered the mainstream, appearing around every corner. It has been applied to the well-managed and also the poorly managed. It has been applied when firms are satisfying their customers as well as when they are failing to serve their customers. It has been applied in its original form and also in adjusted forms that have evolved over the years. And, of course, it has been applied widely beyond the scope of business, to health care, education, and seemingly everything else.

For this reason, my first task in chapter 2 is to define disruption as a phenomenon. In that regard, I want to take it back to its essence, which is that *the phenomenon of disruption occurs when successful firms fail because they continue to make the choices that drove their success.* In other words, it does not apply when firms are poorly managed, complacent, fraudulent, or doing things differently because they are now shielded by barriers to competition. To be sure, firms can fail because of those circumstances, but that is not what we mean by disruption.

In doing this I build up certain terms to describe disruption as a phenomenon. In particular, at its simplest level, what I will term a "disruptive event" occurs when a new product or technology enters the market, causing successful firms to struggle. In chapter 2, I use the example of Blockbuster Video as an anchor case to consider how the concept of disruption and thinking around it evolved. Blockbuster, the successful bricks-and-mortar, global video/DVD rental chain for two decades either side of the 1990s, eventually exited the business in 2010. I will show how its focus on physical retailing prevented it from fully exploiting other online-driven options, not because it was unaware of them or because it failed to experiment with them, but because it was constrained by its historical strategy. However, in doing this, I will show that while many point to Netflix's entry into the market as a disruptive event, it is far from clear that disruption would have been prevented had Netflix not existed. This suggests that the true source of disruptive events can be hard to pinpoint.

In chapter 3, I explore, in full detail, the theories of disruption. There has been a tendency to adopt a single theory as to how disruption might occur: namely, it occurs because new entrants bring in new product innovations at the low end whose improvement ends up felling incumbents that have blind spots. This is the theory proposed by Clayton Christensen, giving rise to the famous prediction that the more a firm is focused on the needs of its traditional customers, the more likely it will fall prey to disruption. Instead, I prefer to term this *the demand-side theory of disruption*, as there is another theory, a *supply-side one*, that also can arise. In the supply-side theory, new innovations are especially difficult for incumbents to adopt and offer competitively because they involve changes in the entire architecture of a product (that is, how components link together) rather than in the components themselves. Consequently, an organization strains most to assimilate new architectural knowledge when it has been successfully focused on exploiting innovations based on the previous architecture. This can be seen in the case of Encyclopaedia Britannica, where that firm's product was based on selling education dreams door to door while the computer brought with it an entirely different approach to supplying those dreams.

The key to dealing with disruption is to understand that it emerges surrounded by uncertainty. While hindsight often suggests that certain disruptive events were obvious, this is far from clear when those events are emerging. Many companies have seen disruption and expended vast resources to deal with it, only to find that disruption was not a threat after all. Others have, of course, failed to see these events until it was too late. In chapter 4, I consider whether disruption can be predicted and also when firms might be naturally in a position to take their time in diagnosing it. For instance, some firms may be shielded from disruptive events because they possess key *complementary assets*, the value of which is not changed and may be enhanced by those events. In doing this, I rely on an influential study of the typesetting industry that underwent four waves of technological change that might otherwise have disrupted incumbents, but in which some firms rode each of those waves because of their library of proprietary fonts.

Because disruption is uncertain, there are two times a firm might choose to deal with it: before the fact (proactively) and after the fact (reactively). In chapter 5, I examine how firms have been able to react to and *manage disruptive events*. The record of successful reactions to disruption was not given much attention by those who proposed theories of disruption, but has been a staple of economic studies of innovation. Those studies indicate that there are reasons why established firms may fail to react to disruptive events: to avoid accelerating the replacement of their own market position and competencies. However, economists have also noted that by dramatically increasing investment in the technologies driving the disruptive event or by acquiring the entrants who were doing so, disruption could be forestalled after the fact. It is true that this is costly for established firms, but it has often meant the difference between stumbling and falling.

Chapters 6 and 7 consider methods that have been proposed to deal with disruption proactively—before such events arise and harm a firm's business. Chapter 6 considers self-disruption, which was proposed by Christensen as a means of proactively avoiding the consequences of demand-side disruption. The idea is that the firm takes control of disruption by charging a new division with the competitive role that would otherwise be taken by a new entrant. This was akin to the position of Britannica's Advanced Technology Group. The chapter highlights several prominent examples of this, including IBM's approach to the personal computer market. These examples demonstrate that while establishing an independent new division can appear to be an effective response, firms often fail to translate it into successful and sustainable models as they kick the dilemmas associated with disruption down the road. Managerial conflicts emerge, and established firms find themselves unable to resolve them effectively.

Chapter 7 then considers how a firm might insure itself against disruption, thereby avoiding the need to respond to it either proactively or reactively. Inspired by Henderson's suggestion with respect to supply-side disruption, I look at integrative approaches that cause firms to be less efficient and competitive overall but allow them to continue to shepherd and assimilate important changes in architectural knowledge. This is akin to the diverse but coordinated approaches used by Matson to integrate old and new approaches to moving goods to, through, and from ships. If a firm wants to ride out continual waves of disruption, it needs to maintain organizational structures that preserve and can evolve architectural knowledge. Integration and continual coordination of component-level teams in product development has been shown to be an effective way to avoid existential threats to successful firms. But what has not been appreciated is that integration and coordination stand diametrically opposed to the independence and self-disruption mantra many firms have adopted to mitigate disruptive risks. *It stands to reason that if your problem is how the parts fit together, adding another unit charged with doing its own thing is not going to solve it.*

Chapter 8 then steps back to reconsider the industry perhaps most famously studied in terms of disruption: the hard disk drive industry. This was the centerpiece of *The Innovator's Dilemma*, but many other academics along with Christensen have studied the industry up to the present day, using the same data. I find that while there was a single disruptive event as hard disk drive suppliers moved to supply personal instead of minicomputers, events that were predicted to be disruptive often did not lead to disruption. Instead, in that industry, one can see the processes of management reaction to disruption—both intense investment by incumbents and acquisitions of entrants—as well as cases where proactive management—featuring both independence and integration—was used to forestall disruption's consequences.

Disruption has been posed as a phenomenon that presents successful businesses with dilemmas. Do they continue to focus on their best customers or pursue a niche that may grow into something more? Do they organize their product teams for rapid innovation or take their time to ensure that the parts fit together? These dilemmas are important, but, when it comes to the existential threats that may arise for established firms, they can be managed. *How* they are managed is perhaps the new and real dilemma facing those firms. Dealing with disruption to ensure a successful and sustainable business involves more than just taking some additional bets with autonomous units that may get you slightly ahead of the game. Instead, this book will show that you need to bake your response to disruption into your mainline organization. The dilemma you face is that betting on sustainability is not without cost to short-run competitive advantage and profitability. Not all businesses will take the same path. However, once you have gone through the journey of disruption—its intellectual history, its practical reality, and the way leaders have dealt with it—you will have the two paths clearly laid out for you. What you do at that point is up to you.

2

What Is Disruption?

Disruption is an overused term rendered almost useless as a conveyer of meaning. However, in its application to business management, it did not start that way. Indeed, in his original work, Christensen used it to mean something very specific, and I believe this meaning provides the right anchor to ground the term. That means that we need to shed the additional baggage that comes with *disruption* as it is used today—especially the notion that the stumbles of every established firm can be classified as consequences of *disruption*. At the same time, however, we need to hold on to the essence of the term: that *disruption* is something that firms that are essentially making historically sound choices may still be at risk of.

To reengineer the term "disruption," I will first set the stage with a recent example—Blockbuster—that people commonly believe encapsulates the phenomenon of disruption (as do I). I will then consider the origins of disruption prior to Christensen's original use of the word. For the purposes of this book, I define disruption as *what a firm faces when the choices that once drove a firm's success now become those that destroy its future*. This will allow us to see disruption as a legitimate phenomenon but also provide a means of distinguishing disruption from other situations that may face a firm.

From Blockbuster to Disaster

If disruption has a modern poster child, it is surely Blockbuster video. In 2004, Blockbuster dominated its US video/DVD rental market (and others around the world) with 9,000 stores, having taken just under two decades to get to that position. By 2010, it had filed for bankruptcy, with its number of outlets shrinking to just a third of its peak number.[1] Blockbuster had gone from success to failure quickly.

Blockbuster was built on the wave of the home video revolution that started in the 1970s and progressed strongly throughout the 1980s, with the videocassette recorder (VCR) becoming a common household product. Video libraries sprang up that allowed people to rent mostly movies at prices that depended on whether the movie was a recent release or not. Blockbuster invested heavily in a global retailing brand that allowed it to dominate the video library market through the 1990s, often using its power to negotiate favorable deals with suppliers of videos and DVDs.

The usual narrative on Blockbuster's failure is a relatively simple one. It began with a technological trigger: the DVD. In the late 1990s, a start-up, Netflix, entered the video rental market on the back of the new DVD standard that was just taking off. Up until that time, if you wanted to rent a movie, you had to travel to a store, select a DVD (or videocassette), watch it, and then return it to the same store. Netflix's idea was to use postal delivery instead. DVDs were lighter and cheaper than their videocassette counterparts, making the idea of postal delivery potentially cost-effective. Crucially, the initial model only appealed to some consumers as it required consumers to plan their DVD watching a few days ahead of time. It also, initially, could not guarantee you the movie you wanted, potentially leaving you high and dry on a Saturday night, though this improved. While the idea of Netflix was motivated by its founder, Reed Hastings, being charged with late fees for video rentals, Netflix initially charged such fees also. In 2000 it changed its business model, moving to a subscription service that allowed consumers to keep DVDs as long as they wanted. In effect, consumers could borrow as often as they could "eat" without thinking beyond a set monthly fee.[2] Consumers loved the new model, and Blockbuster and the bricks-and-mortar video rental industry were doomed.

What makes this a possible story about disruption goes a bit further than the "entrant supplies product(s) that consumers prefer to incumbent" narrative. This is because there were no real constraints that kept Blockbuster from imitating what Netflix did.[3] In hindsight, it didn't have to be destroyed. Indeed, in 2000, Blockbuster decided to pass on the opportunity to buy Netflix for a mere $50 million. (In 2014, Netflix was worth over $26 billion.) In 2002, facing shareholder concerns about Netflix's growth, Blockbuster told them Netflix was not financially viable and was only serving a niche market. By 2004, at the peak of Blockbuster's success, it hedged its bets and offered a DVD-by-mail service with an additional option allowing in-store exchanges. Despite this,

Netflix led in the DVD-by-mail market and never fell back in total subscribers.

I'll return to the Blockbuster story shortly, but it highlights some key aspects of a firm failing because it is being disrupted (rather than for some other reason). First, disruption is often associated with a *new technological opportunity*. In Blockbuster's case it was the DVD and later streaming on the Internet that changed the economics of video delivery and search. We will term this the *disruptive event*. Second, the incumbent often has a *similar ability to exploit the same new opportunity*, though this need not always be the case. (For instance, an entrant may hold a lock-hard patent on the new opportunity or it may require a completely different set of technical know-how that the incumbent does not possess.) Finally, *the failure to take advantage of that opportunity cannot be recovered*. Blockbuster ceded the new business model to Netflix in such a way that there was nothing left of value in Blockbuster's business. As we will see, that does not always occur when new firms enter a market, and there may be something still of value in the incumbent firm, which can mean the difference between being disrupted or not.

Disruption's Origin Story

It is common these days for superheroes to have an "origin story." This is usually a narrative regarding how the hero became super (usually with special powers) but also what gave him or her passion on the road to good rather than evil. Often the story contains a family member or a mentor who plays a critical role in establishing the hero's path. If *disruption* has that figure, his name is Joseph Alois Schumpeter, and he knew it—he even wore a cloak.[4]

Although he ended up a professor in Harvard's economics department, Schumpeter is a far cry from your ivory tower stereotype. He was born and raised in the Austrian aristocracy in the 1880s, held posts around the world including in Egypt, Japan, and later as Austria's finance minister, and proclaimed that his life's goal was to be a great lover, horseback rider, and economist but that he had only achieved two of these.[5] As the Great Depression emerged, Schumpeter was known to have strode, suitably caped, into his Harvard lecture hall, thrilled that the system was getting a cleansing "douche." Suffice it to say that on the modern Internet, such statements would surely have come quickly back to haunt him.

For all his eccentricities, for his academic career Schumpeter was very concerned that capitalism would turn out to be a lot more boring than his predecessors like Karl Marx had described. Schumpeter's early work considered the operation of capitalism as something that, left to ordinary workers and pure owners of capital, would reach a steady state without growth and without anything that looked like profit.[6] Economists then, as now, tended to think of capital goods like machines as earning their own due, but Schumpeter could not imagine a world where people who did nothing but own a machine actually earned a living from it. Those returns would be competed away by the owners of other machines and the competition for workers to operate them. The only people who could generate a profit were those who were generating and then bringing ideas to market: that is, entrepreneurs.

Entrepreneurs are the special heroes in Schumpeter's world, and indeed his image of them lives on in the view of many today. But for all their worth in keeping the system alive and growing, the entrepreneurial reward was itself fleeting. Put simply, an idea, once out there, could be appropriated by many others until the profits from it went away. Thus, we have a picture of entrepreneurial pioneers foraging for transient rewards and, in the process, keeping the system going—although later in life Schumpeter did forecast that those talented individuals would wise up, routinize innovation, and drive the interesting bits of the system away in a corporate malaise.

It was in his 1942 book *Capitalism, Socialism and Democracy* that Schumpeter introduced the concept whose lineage to disruption can be most clearly seen: "creative destruction." Creative destruction is a wonderfully counterintuitive term that many parents would associate with a child at play, learning about the world by tearing it (physically) apart. But, for Schumpeter, it was a description of what he believed to be an endemic feature of capitalism: that the system made room for creativity by destroying what had come before.

Like Marx before him, Schumpeter found evolution rather than equilibrium to be the appropriate narrative for what was occurring in the economy. In fact, the changes from agriculture to industry he saw as "a history of revolutions."

The opening up of new markets, foreign or domestic, and the organizational development from the craft shop and factory to such concerns as U.S. Steel illustrate the same process of industrial mutation—if I may use that biological term—that incessantly revolutionizes the economic structure *from within*, incessantly destroying the old one, incessantly creating a new one. This process of

Creative Destruction is the essential fact about capitalism. It is what capitalism consists in and what every capitalist concern has got to live in.[7]

Unlike the present book, Schumpeter was not trying to explain why successful firms fail. Instead, his goal was to challenge the perception of many economists and certainly politicians at the time, demonstrating that big businesses operating in oligopolistic or monopolistic conditions were not as menacing as many were making them out to be. While he agreed that things looked bad with such firms at any given moment of time, once it was understood that their moment was somewhat fleeting, economists could focus on whether the system was performing well over the long run.

In Schumpeter, we have a picture that has become closer to the modern economist's view of the world. High prices and profits that come from entrepreneurs having a monopoly position in the marketplace are not negative symptoms nor automatically a disease. They are simultaneously the prize for those who have come first to market with an idea and the lure for others to follow. As such, if the system is working as Schumpeter described it, we will have a continual churn in market leadership, though some firms may lead the market for decades. If the system is not working that way, and leaders stay leaders throughout waves of creation, then something is amiss. Nonetheless, this is where the notion was born that success in the capitalist system is precarious, with no natural birthright to a lifelong annuity of profitability.

The Technological Link

While Schumpeter's description of a "gale of creative destruction" identified a key process, he did not explicitly link it to technological changes. Entrepreneurs brought ideas to market, but it was far from obvious that they were the source of the original ideas themselves. Even Schumpeter saw that there were clusters of economic activity at certain points in time which he argued were responsible for business cycles, with significant technological changes driving a more protracted overlay of cycles with bigger booms and busts. By the 1980s, it was obvious to many economists that some firms could hold their positions in industries for many decades, seeming to respond to new technologies and innovations quite well. For example, once Netflix dominated its DVD subscription business, it was able to easily migrate its consumers over to video streaming over the Internet.[8] But, as the Blockbuster example shows, there are other types of innovations that incumbents fail to respond to. The Blockbuster case is interesting because the disruptive innovation that arose was not just triggered by DVDs (a technology Blockbuster adopted) but was, on a broader level, an alternative business model for getting DVDs to consumers. In the generation following Schumpeter, researchers wondered: what types of technological change would spell trouble for incumbents? What types would not?

The natural starting point was to look at "technological discontinuities." The Italian researcher Giovanni Dosi[9] argued that there appeared to be "technological paradigms" that were akin to Thomas Kuhn's "scientific paradigms" and performed a similar role in "changing everything." Sailboat manufacturers, for example, were left in the wind as steam proved faster. Dosi argued that those businesses on the old technological path were focused (as they had to be), but that also made them blind to objectively evaluating the new path.

This notion was reinforced, further developed, and grounded in its implications for innovation strategies for businesses by McKinsey director Richard Foster in a 1986 book.[10] He observed that many broad technologies exhibited an S-curve relationship between effort (whether through labor or capital) devoted to improvements and the rate of improvement in the performance of those technologies on any given metric. S curves are likely familiar to anyone who has read Christensen's work, but I include a brief refresher here.

The shape of the curve refers to the fact that when a technology is new, it takes lots of effort to improve performance even slightly; at some point, however, that relationship flips and small amounts of effort lead to rapid performance improvement. Sadly, this process reaches a conclusion when the relationship eventually flips back, with a plateauing technological limit to performance. While this relationship had been well documented, it was often hard to predict when a takeoff in performance might occur. James Utterback and Bill Abernathy had previously identified the role played by a *dominant design*, explaining that there are opportunities for new entrants up until a set of key technological features becomes the de facto standard.[11] This concept focused the efforts of a diverse set of researchers in improvements, but the phenomenon seemed widespread.

For Foster, combining the S curve with the notion of a technological discontinuity raised an important issue for managers of established firms: it was often the case that a new technology path (representing a new S curve) at first offered lower performance than the existing one. In other

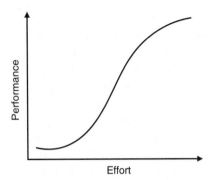

Figure 2.1

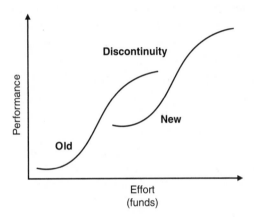

Figure 2.2

words, as an incumbent, you would rationally make a decision to continue to focus on the existing S curve rather than the new. Foster argued that new entrants into an industry were not so encumbered by a past focus and so were more willing to explore the new technology path. If they could do so until the S curve bent upward and could control the technology through that point, the entrants would eventually outcompete the incumbents. That is, if they pursued the new technology with effort, they would take the advantage.

Christensen's Initial Definition

The notion of multiple S curves was the starting point for Clayton Christensen in his initial work, providing an alternative classification of innovations that might generate risks for established firms. Christensen at once both narrowed and expanded Foster's notion. He narrowed it by divorcing it from many preceding theories on technological discontinuities. In particular, Christensen believed that not all technological discontinuities led to *worse* performance by the products of incumbent firms. In fact, some incumbents appeared to have developed radical technological changes that integrated smoothly into their existing products. In other words, a technological discontinuity and a move to a new S curve were not always associated with underperformance as Foster had emphasized. Instead, the change in performance could be upward.

Christensen also dramatically expanded the innovations that may pose risks for incumbents. While his initial work focused on technological changes as precipitating incumbent challenges, Christensen later saw that innovations in the broadest terms (including not only technologies but also new markets and new business models) could pose difficulties for incumbents. Indeed, strictly speaking, his classification evolved to become agnostic as to whether disruption implied a radical technological discontinuity or not.

Christensen saw a particular sort of technology as posing a challenge to established firms, and its definition is instructive:

They ... have two important characteristics: First, they typically present a different package of performance attributes—ones that, at least at the outset, are not valued by existing customers. Second, the performance attributes that existing customers do value improve at such a rapid rate that the new technology can later invade those established markets.[12]

A technology satisfying these criteria was termed by Christensen "disruptive," while all others were considered "sustaining"; that is, they improved the performance of established products.

Thus we see an evolution in the views regarding technology in the disruption line. Schumpeter argued that firms are vulnerable to entrepreneur-based competition. Foster argued that firms would find it difficult to switch to new S curves as this would lead to spells where they underserve their existing customers while in the meantime new entrants, like new species, would secure an advantage on the new S curve. Christensen then saw elements of technologies (and later of other innovations) that would be what he termed "disruptive" by emphasizing the performance gap and rapid performance improvements that may be associated with some technologies but not others.

In *The Innovator's Solution*,[13] Christensen along with Michael Raynor distinguished between two sources of disruptive innovation—low-end and new-market. In low-end disruption, the entrant's product was able to capture some fringe of the customers of the established firms, usually because those customers had been purchasing a product that was too expensive relative to the value they were receiving. New-market disruption occurred when the firm introducing the disruptive innovation was able to capture nonconsumers—customers who had not been consuming the product of established firms at all. However, these two sources are really two sides of the same coin. Prior to the new entry, there is always some consumer who buys from an established firm but retains very little in the way of surplus and so will be that firm's most dissatisfied customer. However, there are also people who were so dissatisfied with what the firm was offering that they were not its customers at all. When a new entrant comes in that can serve either an established firm's most dissatisfied customers or people who were not currently customers at all, the entrant ends up serving both groups in most situations. Thus, the impact of the entrant is similar—it can gain a foothold by coming in at the low end and then can gain traction with the mainline customers of established firms as the technology improves. For that reason, for the purposes of this book I will not distinguish between these two forms of disruptive innovation, focusing instead on the broader difference between disruptive and sustaining innovation. However, I should note that if you are an entrepreneur seeking to enter a market with a disruptive innovation, it is a useful process to think both about who is underserved by established firms and who is poorly served by them. Either way, it is a point of vulnerability for established firms.

Christensen's primary example of a disruptive technology came in the form of new generations of hard disk drives that offered a smaller size but at the initial expense of lower capacity, only to recover that performance gap in a few years. By contrast, the disruptive innovation in DVD rentals is harder to see. For DVD rentals, the performance dimensions were in the product space and positioning rather than in pure technology. Netflix sacrificed the "impulse" nature of DVD rentals that Blockbuster had built its business on, choosing not to compete with the brick-and-mortar outlets that were on every main street. By contrast, Netflix offered a superior outcome to those who were happy to plan their viewing ahead or feared their ability to return DVDs to a store on time. And, initially, this was a niche customer segment in the video rental market, with most consumers continuing their old video renting habit of heading to a local video store.

To complete the story, however, we need to identify where Netflix caught up. Until on-demand video streaming arrived, it did not catch up with regard to impulse viewing; DVDs by post could never satisfy that requirement. But Blockbuster was already having trouble before streaming came to dominate video delivery. Instead, Netflix, like so many online retailers, was able to trump brick-and-mortar outlets on the basis of variety. Netflix could bring viewers the long tail of video content, offering many times more titles than were available in a Blockbuster store. Interestingly, when it did transition to dominance in video streaming, Netflix was often not able to take the most popular new release titles with it. As of the writing of this book, the market for streaming or renting those titles resided elsewhere.[14] It remains to be seen how Netflix's story will play out.

This suggests that, while Christensen's two criteria for a disruptive innovation are easy to describe, it can be difficult to identify precisely whether they have been satisfied in a given case. As we will see below, this issue does add some uncomfortable wrinkles to disruption theory as applied to the Blockbuster case.

Henderson's Alternative Perspective

There is one final chapter in the story of origins of the concept of disruption. At the same time as Christensen was working on his PhD at Harvard, another student, Rebecca Henderson, was interested in the same phenomenon and set forth a research program that ended up having an impact on a generation of management scholars. In fact, Henderson is one of only two Harvard Business School professors to achieve the rank of University Professor (the other being Michael Porter), so it is safe to say that her influence within academic circles has been profound. Perhaps because she has not written popular managerial tomes, she has never had a public profile as a guru. Nonetheless, a reading of her work gives a set of insights that ought to be front and center in the minds of incumbent firm managers.

Henderson was concerned, specifically, with the difficulties incumbent firms had in responding to entrants. For Henderson, it was not so much that those firms chose at critical points not to respond (which was Christensen's focus) but that there were some sorts of technologies or innovations that they couldn't respond to. With her collaborator Kim Clark, she termed these innovations "architectural innovations."

Henderson's variant of disruption theory will be outlined in more detail in the next chapter. For the moment, it is useful to consider her classification of innovations to give a flavor of how they would generate difficulties for successful firms. The way to view this is to consider a "design perspective" on how new products are conceived.

Consider the design of a product as involving a number of components and also how those components are put together (i.e., their architecture). When you develop a new product, you are improving it in certain dimensions: more often than not, new products involve innovations that improve the performance of particular components of existing products. Indeed, this is an efficient way of organizing continual product development, because teams can be tasked with improving components and can work more or less independently of teams in charge of other components. Then their improvements can be slotted together to form a new product. Henderson and Clark pointed out that a fan is made up of blades, motors, a blade guard, control system, and mechanical housing. Each of these are components, but how they are designed to work together is a fan's architecture.

For Henderson, many firms become successful precisely because they can outcompete rivals in product improvements. And the quickest way to do that, perhaps the most efficient in some sense, is to organize for component innovation. But what happens if a new technology comes along that changes the architecture of a product—that is, how the components relate to one another? For successful firms organized around component innovation, thinking about how to recognize and deal with a new architectures is a challenge. Put simply, in an environment that is based on a fixed architecture, how can you even recognize a new architecture when you see it?

So like Christensen, Henderson saw that established firms could, indeed, deal with technological jumps so long as they impacted only specific components. For jumps that involved new architectures, there was a problem. There is a sense in which Netflix's innovation did involve a new architecture. Blockbuster had come to excel in managing inventory and processes in its stores to ensure customers had a satisfactory experience in those stores. However, Netflix was establishing a new logistical approach that could efficiently deliver DVDs directly to people's homes. That involved machinery to sort and deliver DVDs to post offices and then to handle the DVDs as they returned to Netflix. It also required, eventually, a new business model based on subscriptions.

For Blockbuster, its business model defined success by ensuring regular flow through its physical stores. Thus, its entire organization, including the incentives it gave to manage those stores, was designed to ensure that consumers came in and walked out with something, leaving some money behind. To graft an alternative channel onto this organization was difficult, as that channel would not only challenge the economics of the stores (as will be discussed shortly) but also the incentive structures that supported it. This is precisely why new architectures can be more readily brought to market by entrants than incumbents.

We now have two types of innovation that can lead to disruption. What they have in common is that they prove disruptive in the sense of being on a more favorable trajectory than current technologies. To be sure, this does not mean that they are better on all performance dimensions, but that the trajectory allows them to provide products of superior value to consumers relative to the costs of producing them on existing technological paths. Where the two types differ is in their outlook. For Christensen, the innovations are customer-disruptive in that they initially underperform but then rapidly improve performance for an established firm's customers. For Henderson, the innovations are architecture-disruptive in that they initially make it hard to innovate on component improvements but then later allow for rapid improvements as the new architecture is understood.

In this book, I will refer to Christensen-defined customer-disruptive innovation as *disruptive innovation* while Henderson-defined architecture-disruptive innovation is *architectural innovation*. In other words, I'll leave the names as given by their original authors.

In this light, I will show that what Netflix brought into the industry was an innovation that was *both* disruptive *and* architectural. For Blockbuster to respond, it had to be convinced (a) that its current customers wanted what Netflix had to offer and (b) that it should reorganize its entire business to respond to the threat. Suffice it to say that, at the critical times when Blockbuster had to make its decisions, it was not clear to anyone that those conditions had been met. Indeed, the most important common characteristic of both disruptive and architectural innovations may be that when they are first introduced, it is uncertain whether their trajectory for improvement will play out. Put simply, they may offer a new S curve, but that does not necessarily mean it is a better S curve.

When Is a Firm Disrupted?

Armed with a focus on disruption as the phenomenon of successful-firm failure, we should note that there will be aspects of the underlying technology or innovation that will, theoretically at least, both explain the disruption (according to this definition) in the past and allow us to think about its predictive and managerial implications for the future. Disruption begins with a particular event that, through a mechanism, can eventually lead to firm failure. I will refer to this trigger event as the *disruptive event*. The important thing will be to link disruptive events to firm success and failure. Thus, to complete our description of disruption I first need to consider success and failure.

Let's start with failure. Firms fail for all sorts of reasons. In some situations, they fail because of managerial incompetence. For instance, Enron was one of the top ten companies by valuation in the United States and was a poster child for innovativeness in business schools around the world until it suddenly went bankrupt in 2001.[15] However, its failure was due to poor accounting practices and fraud, rather than because of an unmet technological challenge. Firms might also fail because of mismanagement involving a key aspect of a business. This might best be described with reference to the Canadian telecommunications giant Nortel, which the Great Recession finally pushed into bankruptcy and closure in 2009. Nortel had ridden a century-long set of waves of innovation in telecommunications and had become a supplier of leading-edge equipment to networks around the world. The bubble of the late 1990s marked the beginning of its downfall as successive financial irregularities were revealed, accompanied by a revolving door of CEOs. The company was never able to turn its business around despite sitting on a wealth of technical assets and intellectual property that was the subject of intense competitive bidding after its demise.[16]

What Enron and Nortel have in common with Blockbuster is that they were once considered successful firms, or to use Clayton Christensen's word, "great." What makes a firm great is something that we might only know when we see it. To be sure, there are indicators of greatness: high profitability, a large market share, a high stock market valuation, growth, a reputable brand, an aspirational employer. But even for those indicators, we have to ask ourselves: Over what period of time? A firm may grow fast, have high profits, and lead a market, but that leadership may be fleeting—only five years. Or the leadership may last a long time—decades. Or maybe somewhere in between—15 years. What do we regard as sustained success? It is hard to tell.[17] Nonetheless, for many people, Enron, Nortel, and Blockbuster were examples of success.

Where Enron and Nortel differ from, say, Blockbuster is that these firms failed because they were no longer doing what had made them great.[18] Blockbuster, by contrast, had built its business on providing a unified brand for video rental libraries and expanding aggressively in a manner that the famous business historian Alfred Chandler identified as a cornerstone strategy for many of the largest US firms over the past century. When its business declined, it was not because it had stopped doing things like keeping costs down and paying attention to what its customers were doing.

What this implies is that while a firm has to be successful in order to be disrupted, what we consider success must be left fairly open. What is more critical is that disruption occurs when something, whether internal or external, ends up undermining the basis for the success, or, perhaps more accurately, provides a reason why success may have a use-by date.

Undermined by Success

Thus far, we have considered what a disrupted firm might look like and also have described different innovations (disruptive and architectural) that might be trigger events. While it might be possible to look at an industry and all of the innovations that have occurred in it, classify them, and then associate them with the success or failure of incumbents, disruption theory is only complete if we can describe the mechanism that links them. Mere association is not enough.

While the next chapter will explore these mechanisms in more depth, it is worth considering the sketches provided by those who looked at the phenomenon of disruption in the past in order to anchor the definition of disruption I wish to promote.

As already mentioned, for Dosi, who emphasized technological discontinuities, incumbents faced problems in seeing that the old path was doomed and the new path was the future. In his mind, they had organized their businesses around the old path so that moving to the new path was just too hard, whether this was a matter of cost, culture, or managerial myopia. Similarly, for Foster the blind spots of incumbent firms were there because, at the outset, products on the new S curve performed worse than those on the old one and did not initially improve much with effort. For success on a new S curve, fortune favored the bold. Established firms would be reluctant to take that charge, as they had successful existing businesses that still had life in them. By contrast, entrants were not so encumbered and so could take those steps and own the new technological path.

For Christensen, the mechanism was different. While previous approaches had suggested that incumbents just did not see the potential of the new technology, Christensen studied firms that saw the new technological path or innovation, concluding that they evaluated its opportunities using the best business tools at their disposal. This included asking their customers whether they would value the new performance attributes accompanying the innovation. Unfortunately for them, their tools told them to disregard the innovation.

The customer, for Christensen, is central to the story. As already mentioned, a disruptive innovation, by definition, performs worse on many dimensions that existing customers value, while only performing better on some others. Those others have usually been attributes that customers have been taught not to value or have not valued up until that point. (Henry Ford was said to have remarked that if he had asked his customers what they had wanted, they would have said "a faster horse.") For Christensen, the more customer-focused an incumbent actually was, the more likely that it would reject an innovation.

By contrast, for firms that had no customers, that is, for new entrants, the new path was perhaps the only way they could acquire some. Perhaps the entrants were able to find a niche of customers who valued the new performance attributes so much that they were willing to sacrifice the old. Or it could be that they were able to serve people who were not being served by any established firm—perhaps because the innovation was "low-end" and cheaper to implement, or they were addressing a "low-revenue-potential" market. Thus, the fact that the innovation was different and "worse" in some ways was precisely the opportunity for new entrants.[19]

We can see this in the Blockbuster story. What makes this a story of disruption is that the firm in fact faced no barriers that blocked it from competing with Netflix. Netflix's model played off the weaknesses in Blockbuster's own consumer dealings. First of all, late fees, hated by many, were a key and perhaps the main source of Blockbuster's revenue. Netflix aimed to provide a model that did not punish forgetful customers so heavily. Second, while Blockbuster may have thought that consumers enjoyed searching for movies in-store, this search was time-consuming and often left consumers without their preferred movies. Meanwhile Blockbuster had to bear the costs of opening physical stores large enough to house their inventory of popular titles. By being online, Netflix did not have to worry about presenting inventory in a shopping-friendly way. Finally, Netflix could do something Blockbuster could not: offer a wider variety of videos. To be clear, Blockbuster's average customer who had the habit of popping down to the video store on a weekend and was rarely late with returns (and perhaps picked up some snacks as well) might not have gained from Netflix's offering. But there were people who did, and, as Netflix improved, those people became more numerous.

It is the facts that Netflix's entry had an initially slow-moving and peripheral impact on Blockbuster, and that Blockbuster did not respond to that entry, that make this a hallmark example of disruption. Most of Blockbuster's customers were, in fact, happy with their current habits and routines. Many of Netflix's customers were people who were not served by the in-store rental model, perhaps because it was too inconvenient or did not offer them titles of interest. Blockbuster's customers were used to it and had not experienced what a plan-in-advance postal delivery system might be like. Christensen was perhaps right to ask: Would you have acted differently had you been in Blockbuster's shoes?

Another reason why an established firm may not want to adopt a new innovation is that the innovation may cause damage. Blockbuster did, in fact, offer a version of postal delivery that tried to leverage the existence of physical stores (e.g., by allowing in-store exchanges), but there were concerns internally that Blockbuster—the market leader—was legitimizing Netflix's approach and also accelerating consumers' acceptance of postal-based rentals.

Second, and building on this, as already noted Blockbuster was successful because it had optimized the logistics and incentives of physical in-store delivery of videos. This included ensuring that a large number of employees were properly motivated to give customers a great experience. The existence of an uncertain stream of postal delivery and inventory would potentially undermine all of that. For instance, in-store exchanges would be valuable, but how would Blockbuster translate these into incentives for store managers and employees as compared with revenue measures they had been using? Put simply, getting the internal prices right would present a challenge in trying to alter the overall business model. The architectural elements would loom large.

Third, there were real concerns that the new innovation was not viable. For technological changes, it is perhaps easy to evaluate whether they are feasible and will be long-lasting. But for other innovations, especially with regard to business models, it is far from clear that they are economically viable and sustainable. It might well have been that mailing DVDs would become too costly (e.g., due to damage or rising delivery costs). Or perhaps consumers would tire of the subscription model once the novelty wore off. Neither Netflix nor Blockbuster could be sure. For Blockbuster, it would have been costly to integrate a new product into its business only for it to turn out not to be a successful innovation after all, let alone a disruptive one. Perhaps, for established firms, it is more useful to adopt a wait-and-see attitude.[20]

But why is waiting and seeing not always a viable option? To complete the link between disruptive innovation and great-firm failure, there has to be a reason why the great firm fails to adopt an innovation once it is clear that it is performing well across all attributes—including those traditionally valued by its own customers. Netflix grew so rapidly that Blockbuster was never able to recover. Essentially, the business it was trying to preserve was no longer worth much. Here's Christensen on the subject:

Blockbuster's mistake? To follow a principle that is taught in every fundamental course in finance and economics. That is, in evaluating alternative investments, we should ignore sunk and fixed costs, and instead base decisions on the marginal costs and revenues that each alternative entails. But it's a dangerous way of thinking. Almost always, such analysis shows that the marginal costs are lower, and marginal profits are higher, than the full cost.[21]

What he is saying here is that Blockbuster was too limited in its view: it had miscalculated the extent to which its existing business had lost value. Poor thinking, Christensen goes on, "biases companies to leverage what they have put in place to succeed in the past, instead of guiding them to create the capabilities they'll need in the future." In my mind, Blockbuster's problem was not so much that it ignored sunk and fixed costs but that it didn't do so. It was concerned with how moving away from physical stores would impact on the performance of the stores it had already set up. Christensen suggests that what ultimately put the nail in the coffin for established firms are biases toward the old and against the new. In that regard, it is not too different from the mechanisms put forward by Dosi and Foster. What is different in disruption theory is the type of innovations that make those "biases" a path to failure for established firms.

There is, however, a final wrinkle in the Blockbuster story that sets it apart from the simple notion that it was encumbered by its bricks when responding to Netflix. Netflix became a successful firm on the back of a "soon to be outdated" technology, the DVD. The DVD was also the bread and butter of Blockbuster's business, although it could also sell consumers popcorn (or corn and butter). It was the transition to a newer technology—Internet streaming—that brought the long-envisioned dream of on-demand video to households. Netflix introduced its streaming service in 2007 as an add-on to its DVD subscription business.

YouTube was launched the same year, Hulu shortly after, and then cable companies got into the on-demand mix.

Blockbuster, however, has its own on-demand story. It actually experimented with several services through the first decade of the millennium. In one of these, consumers bought a $100 box that could attach to their televisions (something that has proved a stable model these days).[22] As early as 2000, Blockbuster launched its own on-demand movie rental service over the Internet.[23] However, the trial which ran in four US states did not work out. It was not clear whether there was a lack of content, the technology didn't work well enough, or customers were not ready to adopt yet, but the problem likely was a lack of broadband penetration coupled with a $5 charge that was more expensive than in-store rentals. Then again, perhaps Blockbuster, which needed to partner to develop the technology required for this service, chose the wrong ally. Who had financed and promoted this new path for Blockbuster? As it turns out, it was Enron, perhaps in hindsight not the most reliable partner.[24]

Disrupted by Success

We thus arrive at a solid description of the phenomenon of disruption. Successful firms that are disrupted are not complacent or poorly managed. Instead, they continue on the path that brought them to success. It is precisely because this is an appropriate thing for them to do that they are disrupted. How this can happen is what we will explore in the next chapter.

It is very easy to believe that Blockbuster was brought down by one disruptor, Netflix. But consider the following counterfactual exercise: Had Netflix not existed, would Blockbuster's story have been much different?

There is a case to be made that it would have been much the same. Netflix was one of a number of services that brought on-demand video products to the marketplace. Its only difference was that it had a customer base used to regular monthly payments from their DVD service. The same thing could have been said of cable companies which today command a large share of the on-demand market. This would have disrupted Blockbuster had Netflix not done so, in much the same way as its focus on supporting the physical infrastructure for in-store delivery was always an anchor on its choices even as it experimented with newer technologies.

Perhaps Blockbuster could have purchased Netflix at an earlier opportunity. However, again this would have been done to slow the impact on its physical retailing business. It could have taken out a competitor in this way, but it is far from clear that the outcome would have been any different from our thought experiment in which Netflix did not exist. In any case, the price was never right and that deal for Netflix was never done.

In the end, a deal was instead done *for* Blockbuster. In 2011, Dish Network (a large satellite broadcasting provider) purchased Blockbuster for $320 million, an amount less than its annual late-fee revenues when Netflix was gaining initial traction.[25] Blockbuster actually lives on as a brand with Dish's Blockbuster On Demand service today. From a giant to a brand on a broadcasting channel, the Blockbuster case reveals many of the nuances related to disruption.

3

Sources of Disruption

Rarely can we point to an exact moment in history when a major technological advance with an extraordinarily widespread impact took place. One of those rare moments occurred on January 9, 2007, when Apple CEO Steve Jobs introduced the world to the very first iPhone at the annual MacWorld conference. While it would not be released for another six months, the iPhone captured the attention of everyone from the technorati to the mainstream press.[1] The iPhone transformed the mobile phone industry, consigning even the most impressive advances made by incumbents up until then to ancient history. Moreover, as that transformation took place, many of mobile's leading lights—Nokia, Sony-Ericsson, Motorola, and BlackBerry—effectively failed.[2]

Interestingly, this was roughly a decade after Christensen had released his major work on disruption, and the iPhone launch sparked confusion about whether or not it was an example of disruption theory in action. The iPhone led to the failure of successful firms, but there seemed to be incompatible nuances in this case; specifically, Apple actually entered at the high end of the mobile handset market rather than at the low end, which, as I will explain, was normally the way disruption was thought to arise.

Here I will contend that this confusion stems from not appreciating *all* of the sources of disruption. To properly understand the iPhone and disruption, we need to investigate the theoretical mechanisms by which a particular type of technology may cause incumbent firms to be disrupted. I will outline two sources of disruption, based on disruptive or architectural innovations respectively. First, there is a *demand-side* mechanism that emerged from Christensen's work, suggesting that established firms can be blindsided by certain types of innovations that change what products their customers want, ultimately leading to the established firms' failure. Second, there is a *supply-side* mechanism that emerged from Henderson's work suggesting that, for certain innovations, successful incumbents may not be able to make the organizational changes necessary to compete with new entrants.

I will use the iPhone-championed changes in the mobile handset industries since 2007 as an anchor point for this discussion. In particular, I will evaluate whether, in fact, the iPhone was a disruptive innovation or not, examining the subtlety of how it fits into both demand-side and supply-side theories. This will demonstrate the full picture of the iPhone's disruptive consequences.

Was the iPhone a Disruptive Innovation?

The first step to understanding whether the iPhone was an example of a disruptive innovation is to evaluate whether it fits the criteria. Recall that a disruptive innovation is one that initially performs worse on characteristics that most consumers value and then rapidly improves its performance on those characteristics, causing it to become a market leader. This definition presents some challenges to evaluation, as it is only possible in hindsight to determine whether an innovation manages to meaningfully improve. This explains why many who observed the inaugural iPhone launch had trouble evaluating it. For example, in 2007 Christensen, like many others at the time, did not see the iPhone as a disruptive innovation and predicted that Apple would fail to be an effective competitor:

The iPhone is a sustaining technology relative to Nokia. In other words, Apple is leaping ahead on the sustaining curve [by building a better phone]. But the prediction of the theory would be that Apple won't succeed with the iPhone. They've launched an innovation that the existing players in the industry are heavily motivated to beat: It's not [truly] disruptive. History speaks pretty loudly on that, that the probability of success is going to be limited.[3]

Whereas Christensen believed that the iPhone was a better rather than a worse product for consumers, incumbents saw the iPhone very differently. Pekka Pohjakallio (Vice President, Nokia): "They had music, internet, an email deal with Yahoo and a deal with Google, but it is a 2G device, not 3G, which was a surprise to me."[4] Mike Lazaridis (founder, RIM): "Try typing a web key on a touchscreen on an Apple iPhone, that's a real challenge. You cannot see what you type."[5] Lazaridis and Pohjakallio were objectively right—the first iPhone did indeed perform worse as a phone and even as an Internet communication device based on traditional specs (it did not even have the industry-standard keyboard!).

Indeed, plenty of commentators in 2007 said that Apple had no chance in the market.[6] This shows the challenge of evaluating whether a new innovation is a disruptive innovation or not. Given the initially worse performance of the iPhone on key dimensions that mobile phone consumers valued, and the ability of Apple to improve it rapidly, it would appear in hindsight to fall into the strictly defined category of a customer-disruptive innovation. However, the incumbents in the industry seem not to have recognized its potential. The leaders of BlackBerry, for example, continued for years to maintain that Apple would not be a threat as their customers wanted a physical and tactile keyboard.[7]

The Demand-Side Theory of Disruption

Having evaluated in hindsight that the iPhone had the characteristics of a disruptive innovation, I now will explore in detail the first of two broad mechanisms that can link a disruptive event to the disruption of established and successful firms. The demand-side theory comes from Christensen and his description of the risk that established firms face. The idea is that established firms fail to react to new-entrant innovation not because they are unaware of it but rather because, through standard and sensible analysis, they come to the opinion that their customers (comprising most of the market) would not want what the entrant is offering. Trouble comes when it turns out that this assessment is incorrect and too nearsighted. In fact, there is more than trouble, as the established firm is blindsided and, according to Christensen, often has no options for recovering its leading position at that point.

This is perhaps the most memorable theoretical proposition from Christensen's first book, so much so that it is worth using his words. Having outlined how many firms that were once great later found trouble, Christensen wrote:

Good management was the most powerful reason they failed to stay atop their industries. Precisely *because* these firms listened to their customers, invested aggressively in new technologies that would provide their customers more and better products of the sort they wanted, and because they carefully studied market trends and systematically allocated investment capital to innovations that promised the best returns, they lost their positions of leadership.[8]

It is no wonder then that Intel CEO Andy Grove described the book as "scary." Managers could be blindsided by their own customer focus. The implication of this statement was not lost on the book's readers nor on Christensen, as he explained that many "now widely accepted principles of good management" are only appropriate in certain situations. In particular, there are times when it is "*right* not to listen to customers, right to invest in developing lower-performance products that promise *lower* margins, and right to aggressively pursue small, rather than substantial, markets." In other words, the implication of the theory is that a seemingly irrational management decision may be a good one. With those managerial implications—which I will return to in a later chapter—it is worth exploring more deeply the conditions that give rise to the demand-side theory.

The key moment of interest is when a firm understands that a new technology has emerged with some superior characteristics appealing to a niche of consumers, and must decide whether to pursue it. In *The Innovator's Dilemma*, Christensen argued that if, at that point, the company relies on its current decision-making processes—on the very approach that has made it successful in the past—things will go awry and will, in a sense, be irrecoverable. This is particularly the case when it comes to translating what customers want into actionable items within the organization. In effect, he saw that once the decision touched the usual procedures, the organization would move along a set path that accommodated the preferences of people it depended on. While many people provide resources to companies (most notably investors), Christensen saw the firm's current customers as its primary crutch.[9] All of an organization's procedures and routines are geared toward serving them, and thus it is hardly surprising that, like a reaction to a foreign virus, the organization would reject proposals that would harm these customers. Note how this fits into the theory of disruption as I have defined it: the very thing that makes an organization successful—gearing itself toward the needs of its customers—hinders it in making the appropriate decision regarding a new technology or other innovation.

It is useful to consider the reaction of Research In Motion (or RIM, as BlackBerry was known at the time) to the iPhone announcement. RIM's co-founder Mike Lazaridis immediately called an "all-hands meeting" just days after Jobs's announcement.[10] Thus, he engaged the organization as a whole in deciding how to respond to the iPhone. They came to the conclusion that while the new operating system was elegant and well designed, RIM had been built on solid hardware.

Lazaridis had long respected Apple's design acumen. But, he said, "Not everyone can type on a piece of glass. Every laptop and virtually every other phone has a tactile keyboard. I think our design gives us an advantage." Superior hardware would win out, he believed.[11]

As already noted, externally RIM portrayed an image of unconcern. Internally, its engineering team set to work on analyzing what it would take to produce a competing device. The answer was that it would be hard to do what it currently did without compromising on size (a bulkier phone), battery life, and RIM's general belief that networks could not handle the bandwidth. Indeed, BlackBerry's entire success in building a reliable connected device had been based on economizing on bandwidth using its own proprietary network solution. The resounding answer the company leadership threw back was that its customers would not accept the tradeoffs implied by the iPhone. Thus RIM stayed with its traditional course rather than embarking on a multiyear project to revamp its operating system.[12]

While it is tempting with the benefit of hindsight to be amused by these choices, it is important to note that, over the next two years, RIM's view of the world was largely confirmed. In fact, sales of BlackBerries increased as consumers saw how favorably they compared in price to Apple's option. The rising tide was lifting all boats as consumers moved from existing "dumb" phones to smarter phones. In 2009, RIM was named the fastest-growing company in the world by *Fortune* magazine, and its core customer base of government and business enterprises remained a solid source of support. Its subscriber based continued to grow through 2011.

We see here precisely what makes the notion of disruption so compelling: that successful firms can fail by doing the *very things* that have made them successful. If the iPhone launch was the disruptive event for RIM, then it took more than two years for the actual disruptive impact to show up. Over that period, the alternative hypothesis—that the iPhone would not be the success that it turned out to be—had significant evidentiary support. We will return to consider managerial responses in a later chapter, but it is important to emphasize here that there will always be considerable *uncertainty* about whether an event has been disruptive or not.

There is another possibility here, which to my knowledge has never been explored: namely, that the iPhone launch itself was not the disruptive event for RIM, Nokia, Sony-Ericsson, and Motorola. Apple did not proceed as a standard disruptor. Instead, the iPhone was priced at the high end of the market, with a higher price than almost all of its competitors.[13] Apple, in fact, asked consumers to sacrifice features and pay more for the privilege. What is more, they remained on the more expensive side of the market thereafter. This is not to say that Apple wasn't providing competition; but that alone would not have pushed the incumbents out. As we saw from the RIM story, the iPhone launch at first actually improved consumers' perceptions of the value of the BlackBerry as more affordable and of more established quality.

This highlights an important missing element in the demand-side theory as expounded by Christensen—the impact of price.[14] This element was noted by Dartmouth professor Ron Adner in 2002, who tried to make sense of Christensen's story using the formal language of economic theory.[15] Adner began by trying to think of a product as a bundle of characteristics rather than a single product per se. This was an approach developed decades earlier by Kevin Lancaster and allowed economists to understand the relationship between product design and demand. For Adner, he imagined that established firms had a product that, for example, emphasized attribute A (longer battery life) rather than attribute B (a larger screen). He wondered under what circumstances an entrant, developing a product with different emphases, would get traction in the market. For instance, if it turned out that consumers who liked longer battery life did not care for a larger screen and vice versa, then both incumbent and entrant could coexist in the market. But what if, instead, there was some set of consumers who were more willing to compromise on both dimensions? In that situation, the old product—which had long worked on developing increasing battery life—would reach diminishing returns in terms of consumer value. By contrast, the newer product would have considerable room for improvement. In this situation, for compromising customers, the entrant might have an edge.

While this sounds like potential trouble for the incumbent, there was one final wrinkle identified by Adner. Even though this set of customers might tip toward the entrant because they were willing to compromise, they were going to care more about price in making their choices. Thus, if the entrant (in our case Apple) entered with a higher price, the incumbent (RIM) would be able to defend its main turf from invasion, resulting in more competition but no doom. But if, instead, the entrant found a way to make the product cheaper, the tables would be turned, putting the incumbent in a precarious position. The incumbent, having already reached the limits of how it could create nonprice value (through longer battery life), would end up ceding significant ground.

This highlights a core element of the demand-side theory of disruption that was noted but not explained by Christensen. For a blindside to occur, the theory requires that an entrant come in at the low end, appealing to a niche group of consumers who are willing to sacrifice on certain features available in other products. It is precisely because disruptors enter at the low end that their lower prices allow them to eventually capture consumers from incumbents. This, coupled with Adner's S-curve relationship that held not on performance per se but on the *value* of characteristic level of performance to consumers, completed the theory as to how a disruptive innovation could displace a successful incumbent.

So if Apple, with its higher-priced iPhone, was not a true disruptor, what then happened to established mobile handset manufacturers? There was, in fact, a low-end entrant and disruptor in the form of Google's Android phones. In 2007, Google immediately saw what it was dealing with, given the iPhone.

Chris DeSalvo's reaction to the iPhone was immediate and visceral. "As a consumer I was blown away. I wanted one immediately. But as a Google engineer, I thought 'We're going to have to start over.' ... What we had suddenly looked just so ... nineties," DeSalvo said. "It's just one of those things that are obvious when you see it."[16]

The first Android phones were still vastly inferior to the iPhone and other mobile phones, but they were substantially cheaper and positioned at the low end. Combined with Google's strong incentives to proliferate the platform for other reasons (e.g., supporting its advertising revenues) and virtually give the operating system away, this drove the price down further.[17]

But a puzzle remains: given that Google was partnering with phone makers to develop Android phones, why were the phone makers who took the lead with Android not the incumbents in the industry? Instead, it was Samsung, HTC, and LG (and initially Motorola), which were themselves new entrants in the smart-phone industry at the time, and even they were late movers relative to the iPhone. Thus, surely there was ample opportunity for the established manufacturers to come back after initially missing the iPhone boat. After Android gained traction, however, RIM's market share and sales started to decline to the point of layoffs. RIM's brand was suffering, considered out of date, and the patience of investors was wearing thin. RIM seemed not so much blindsided as bogged down.[18]

The demand-side theory of disruption says that if technologies that emerge have low initial performance but rapid improvement, this should be associated with incumbent firm failure. If firm failure is not observed, this would count against the theory. We have seen, however, that the innovation must be brought to market at the low end to be consistent with the demand-side theory—hence allowing us to dismiss the iPhone as the consequential disruptive event for established mobile handset makers. But we are also left with a puzzle. The demand-side theory of disruption says that the new technology leads to established-firm failure as these firms do not have time to recover. In the iPhone case, however, there was time, as evidenced by the delayed entry and subsequent market capture and growth of low-end smart phones based on Android. Moreover, these handset manufacturers offered a variety of products including variants of smart phones. Why did those phones not succeed as the less-established or, indeed, new entrants were able to do?

Dominant Designs

At this juncture, as we move from the demand-side to the supply-side theory of disruption, it is useful to revisit a very long-standing concept in the theory of technological change and management: that of the *dominant design*. I already mentioned this 1970s concept, developed by James Utterback and Bill Abernathy, when describing the S-curve relationship between effort and performance. The emergence of a dominant design is often at the heart of the steep, accelerating part of this curve, where something akin to a standard way of doing things emerges in an industry, and this focuses the attention of innovators on improving the way that design works rather than experimenting with fundamentally alternative designs. For instance, automobiles had been around for decades before Ford's Model T, striking the right balance between speed, body shape, and modular components, could be assembled cost-effectively on a production line. Similarly, prior innovations led up to the DC-3 manufactured by Douglas, a plane that was neither large, fast, nor capable of the longest ranges but struck the right economic balance between those things. All passenger aircraft design for 25 years coalesced around this design until the emergence of jet aircraft, which allowed the costs of production to drop dramatically.[19]

I raise the concept of dominant design here because it helps us understand the disruptive event that took place in the mobile handset industry. While there were some standard elements to handset design prior to the iPhone, there was considerable variety in the user interface designs. What the iPhone did was create a smart-phone design that became the standard for what followed on a number of dimensions. The bricklike hardware design with a full-length touch screen and minimal buttons on the device stood in great contrast to many of the earlier design decisions. Though the now-ubiquitous icon table for apps had existed in devices before the iPhone, including the Palm Pilot and the BlackBerry, it was the integration of gestures and the very notion that the phone function was just one of many apps, rather than the primary reason for owning the device, that changed the industry. Most phones ever since have followed this style of user interface and phone handling; an exception perhaps is the Windows phone that does not use icons as a point of entry for users.[20]

This aspect of the user interface provided a standard for app designers to work with too. Prior to the Apple interface, app designers had to design for multiple functions (e.g., the availability of buttons and keyboards) that ranged across the numerous different phones. From 2008, that was an irrelevant exercise, as there were no buttons. Instead, Apple provided tools that reinforced standard icons, gestures, and layout to ensure that the user interface was familiar to users, giving designers constraints while reducing the cost of "teaching the user" how to relate to their app. Suffice it to say that, in five or so years, across a number of platforms, a million new apps appeared out of nowhere.

We can view the dominant design in mobile handsets as the disruptive event rather than one particular product or innovation. Of course, this still leaves open the issue as why the established handset manufacturers were unable to exploit this design as Apple, Samsung, LG, and HTC did, especially since customers had adopted the new dominant design widely. For this reason, it strikes me as implausible that the demand-side theory of disruption could account for what happened to Nokia, BlackBerry, and the like.

The Supply-Side Theory of Disruption

We turn now from the customer to the organization of established firms. Organizationally, what makes many firms successful is that they develop processes, routines, and capabilities that allow them to continue to engage in both product and process innovation in a systematic way. Economists consider these firms to be "optimizing"—that is, organizing themselves in the best way to fit the current or anticipated future environment. On that basis, it might seem that disruption is unlikely ever to occur, because such firms could seamlessly adjust to any potential disruptive event. However, the process of optimization is a difficult one and in particular is a difficult one to adjust. Armin Alchian and Milton Friedman suggested in the 1950s that firms can act *as if* they are profit maximizers even if they find it hard to adjust to change, so long as competitive selection works to weed out those who are not making as much profit and boost those who are.[21]

Successful established firms often command a degree of market power that makes them immune to displacement if the suboptimizations that occur as a result of adjusting their processes are small, but not if they are large. Many who study management have become intensely interested in why established firms might fail to adjust quickly enough and how to manage such adjustment in a proactive manner.

It is from this tradition that a supply-side theory of disruption emerges.[22] Let's start this supply-side description by returning to the iPhone. The puzzle with regard to the iPhone is not that people within incumbent firms did not understand its potential (regardless of initial public pronouncements) or that phones that were competitive with it could not be produced outside of Apple (as they were by Samsung and HTC). Indeed, even after a few years in the market, Apple had far from a dominant or even a majority share of the new touch-based smart phones being sold globally. The key question instead is why it was the new entrants into the mobile phone industry rather than incumbents who took charge. What might explain why incumbents cannot simply adopt entrant innovations?

While it is perhaps tempting to think of incumbent firms as slow-moving, not broad enough in their thinking (either laterally or into the future), and overly political in their decision making, those things can explain sluggishness but not paralysis in the face of impending catastrophic doom. Instead, theories of incumbent inaction tend to delve deeper: arguing that it is precisely what made those firms great in the past that generates a sclerosis when they need to change.

One version of this theory focuses on information channels and communication structures. In 1974, hot on the heels of winning a Nobel prize, Kenneth Arrow penned an influential book called *The Limits of Organization*.[23] He saw the organization as comprised of individuals with a limited ability to absorb and communicate information. As organizations had to process information all the time—bringing information from the people who have it to the people who need it for decisions—they developed processes, routines, and other procedures to economize on the costs of all that communication. Arrow termed this an organizational "code." A code is like a language. It is very efficient and can be created to optimize itself for the circumstances at the time—which is why organizations with the right code can do very well in complex environments—but at the same time it is hard to change. People are encouraged to buy in to the code, which means that if one needs to change how communication flows, one must coordinate that change across many individuals. Arrow's thesis is that such coordination may be so hard that only a large clearing of the decks, perhaps through generational change, could do the job.[24]

While the notion of a code resonates, in its stark theoretical form it is a pessimistic view of how much change firms might be able to accommodate. Nonetheless, it provides a starting point for understanding the supply-side theory of disruption. Some codes serve an organization well but perhaps have a use-by date. It was Rebecca Henderson and Kim Clark who drew the connection between this and how companies go about innovation. According to them, one must consider two types of knowledge that might flow through an organization: *component knowledge* and *architectural knowledge.*

Making a product, particularly a high-tech one, requires people with specialized skills and training. No one could design and build a modern airliner on their own, but an entire team could build it. To do so, collaborative team employees possess and work on improving their component knowledge—knowledge that can be generated at the level of one or just a few individuals. For a mobile device, companies will have teams working on the battery, input screen, casing, radio antenna, microprocessor, and memory. All such devices have these components, and over time successful established companies will become better at delivering them at higher quality and lower cost. Critically, it is by organizing themselves to achieve such improvements that successful firms can maintain their competitive advantage. Not surprisingly, therefore, their codes—the way the teams talk to each other—are often optimized to achieve this end: to allow teams to focus on what they know and minimize the need for cross-team exchanges.

But the teams can never operate purely independently. At some level, knowledge must be generated that establishes how their components are linked and the impact of changes in one component on the performance of others. That is, within the organization, there is a need for architectural knowledge that conveys how all the pieces fit together.

While the process by which component knowledge is acquired and improved seems quite transparent and somewhat obvious—akin to Schumpeter's lament that the process of innovation might become routine—the forming of architectural knowledge is harder to pinpoint. The best theories imagine that an organization, at some undefined stage in its evolution, experiments with different ways of putting components together to make a product. At some point, a dominant design emerges that both manages tradeoffs between components and also sets standards that should be adhered to regarding any one component's impact on others. From there on, the firm organizes itself around that architectural knowledge. In some sense, it is imprinted on or embedded within the firm's structure. This is a huge boost as continual innovation can proceed apace without having to rely on any one individual. Thus architectural knowledge in firms is not codified in a way that can be communicated easily but is tacit, like the unspoken seating arrangements of attenders at a regular meeting.

We see here the ingredients of a supply-side theory of disruption. Successful firms ride a set of architectural knowledge; the decision makers in the firm can take that knowledge as given and move on to organizing for improvements in component knowledge. This is wonderfully efficient and leads to a smoothly operating firm—but at the same time, there is a specter of doom. What if that architectural knowledge itself becomes obsolete?

It is at this point that we can understand Henderson and Clark's approach. In a 1990 article they explicitly related the success or failure of incumbent firms to whether they needed to engage in architectural and component innovation. This particular classification offers what we would term today a "design perspective" on how new products are conceived.

How the components of a mobile device are put together can differ from device to device. Many have noted that the iPhone did not use radically new components. While it is hard to look at older mobile phones and iPhones as the same class of experience for consumers, my belief is that fundamentally they were. You still had a screen and, despite the fact that the buttons had migrated to the screen, the user interaction was familiar. Moreover, the evolution to include a music player and email was obvious. Arguably, Apple's iPhone therefore represented an architectural innovation. Apple had designed a new way of putting those components together.

The Henderson-Clark theory is that incumbent firms are great at supplying component innovations but may be unable to adopt architectural innovations. Why is this so? As already noted, the reason lies in such knowledge being deeply embedded within the firm.

Architectural innovation presents established firms with a more subtle challenge. Much of what the firm knows is useful and needs to be applied in the new product, but some of what it knows is not only not useful but may actually handicap the firm. Recognizing what is useful and what is not, and acquiring and applying new knowledge when necessary, may be quite difficult for an established firm because of the way knowledge—particularly architectural knowledge—is organized and managed.[25]

The Henderson-Clark theory is that architectural knowledge is something that is fundamentally hidden from view. Consequently, outsiders do not know where to start to generate a similar product with a similar architecture.

But why then can new entrants do better than incumbents at launching products with a new architecture? One reason is that the codes an incumbent firm develops are specialized toward a previous architecture and cannot be changed easily. With respect to the iPhone this has some resonance. Within a few years, incumbents offered their own versions of touch screen phones that could offer apps, but in each case they were still expensive and also appeared to lag behind the iPhone in terms of quality. They thought they could counter the iPhone on the basis of their existing components (particularly operating systems) but instead failed to gain traction in the market. Incumbent firms did not see that the iPhone represented an architectural change rather than a component one.

Even if a firm does recognize an innovation as architectural, it has to deal with the issue of how to replicate the new architecture. Arguably, for example, Android phones have never quite replicated the iPhone experience in terms of quality. More fundamentally, learning how to develop products with a new architecture requires an entirely new mode of learning. It is natural for incumbents to consider some of their old knowledge—of both architecture and components—as relevant, but this makes them hesitate before adopting changes that make that knowledge irrelevant.[26]

Accounts of how firms have dealt with architectural innovations generate a pessimistic view for their managers:

The problems created by an architecture innovation are evident in the introduction of high-strength-low-alloy (HSLA) steel in automobile bodies in the 1970s. The new materials allowed body panels to be thinner and lighter but opened up a whole new set of interactions that were not contained in existing channels and strategies. One automaker's body-engineering group, using traditional methods, designed an HSLA hood for the engine compartment. The hoods, however, resonated and oscillated with engine vibrations during testing. On further investigation, it became apparent that the traditional methods for designing hoods worked just fine with traditional materials, although no one knew quite why. The knowledge embedded in established problem-solving strategies and communication channels was sufficient to achieve effective designs with established materials, but the new material created new interactions and required the engineers to build new knowledge about them.[27]

This suggests that responding to architectural innovation has a bleak prospect, but it also gives us insight into why incumbent mobile phone manufacturers had so much difficulty in generating new products with the new architecture—ceding large and irrecoverable market share before they were able to do so.

The supply-side theory of disruption gives us a complete picture as to why the iPhone's introduction/Android follow-on was a disruptive event that eventually led to the failures of many established mobile handset manufacturers while the new entrants grew. The iPhone created a major leap in classic architectural innovation. Established manufacturers were not set up to deal with the departure from the component focus that had made them so successful in the past. In particular, the integration of software and hardware was a new, difficult issue. For instance, Mike Lazaridis, the technical genius behind the BlackBerry, had always pushed for hardware to be durable and efficient in its energy and network use. To do this, he wanted the mobile device to do one thing (text communication and email) well.[28] However, that vision was at odds with the notion that a handheld device would evolve into a mobile computer. And, for that, software was key—from the operating system to the app ecosystem that developed around it.

In order to deal with the iPhone, incumbents would have had to recognize the innovation as architectural, as Google did. Incumbent organizations were never set up to see new innovations that way. Instead, no doubt each team examined the iPhone and subsequent Android devices on their own component merits, saw that there were no significant advances, and could comfortably tell those higher up that they could replicate the components at will. That was likely the case. But they couldn't replicate how these things were put together—not without root-and-branch change throughout the organization. But in this fast-paced industry, there was no time left for that.

Anticipating the Managerial Issues

This chapter has outlined both the demand-side and supply-side theories of disruption. Demand-side disruption can arise when firms that are customer-focused continue to pay attention to their customers without realizing that entrants, who begin with other, underserved customer segments, have technological trajectories that will eventually become a serious competitive threat. Supply-side disruption can arise when firms that have become intensely focused on improving components of an existing architecture are unable to respond when entrants are able to innovate on a new and ultimately more promising architecture. Of course, these two theories of disruption are not mutually exclusive, as both, only one, or neither may be supported by the evidence in a particular case, something I will examine in the next chapter. But it is instructive to note here that they involve potentially different managerial issues.

There are two ways an incumbent can deal with disruption. The first way is, when a disruptive event arises, to recognize it and do something about it. Both the demand-side and supply-side theories, however, seem to suggest that this type of *reactive management* approach is often fruitless. For the demand-side theory, it would involve a difficult adjustment away from satisfying current customers until subsequent improvements bring them back again. For the supply-side theory, adjustment may not be possible, as architectural knowledge cannot be embedded into an organization with a deeply ingrained integration of past knowledge. Though both theories appear to imply that managerial decision making can be supplanted by the tide of events, to properly explore this we need to consider alternative forms of reactive management and see how effective they might be in regard to both demand- and supply-side disruptive events.

The second way to deal with disruption is through *proactive management*, whereby managers, before disruptive events take place, move to insure their organization against them. Here the demand- and supply-side theories offer very different prescriptions. Proactive management on the demand side requires creating an organization with autonomous divisions that can work independently of others—so as, for instance, to serve niche customer segments while not being limited by the profit focus of divisions serving primary customer segments. By contrast, proactive management on the supply side requires creating a more integrated, fluid organization so that there is a reduced focus on component knowledge and a recognition and nurturing of new architectural knowledge. Given the two different theoretical approaches to proactive management against disruption, organizations will always face a hard choice between them. How to make this tradeoff will become clearer as we investigate the evidence and relative merits for both demand- and supply-side theories of disruption.

4

Predicting Disruption

The history of technology is littered with examples of insiders who failed to see a technology's potential as it emerged in their own backyard. AT&T lawyers, for example, famously declined to patent the laser developed by Bell Labs (AT&T's research arm) because there were no apparent applications to telephony.[1] A couple of decades later, lasers were at the heart of the system of optical fiber technology linking the world. In a similar case, Bell Labs was again part of a team (the Moving Pictures Experts Group or MPEG) that in the mid-1990s developed an audio compression format that dramatically reduced the size of digital files containing music: the MP3 format. Music publishers at the time did not embrace the new standard as it resulted in lower sound quality than the prevailing standard of compact disks. In fact, a few years later, when Napster and other online MP3 music-sharing services emerged, music publishers took to fighting the MP3 standard rather than adopting it.[2] Audience preference for the convenience of MP3 music, however, continued to grow, and today almost all music sold online is compressed in an MP3 (e.g., on Amazon) or similar format (e.g., MP4 on iTunes).

Stories such as these ended up seeping into the lore surrounding disruption—particularly demand-side disruption. In each case, a new technology was developed with either a nonobvious application to a key industry or worse performance than the existing technology on a seemingly key dimension. In each case, that new technology eventually took over the industry. Interestingly, however, neither of these examples had a disruptive outcome: by the time the value of laser technology to telecommunications was obvious, it had developed to become a better-performing technology and as such was ready for adoption by incumbents in the industry. Similarly, compressed music never surpassed less-compressed alternatives in sound quality, but its ability to be disseminated online opened up a new form of distribution that changed the industry standard for both incumbents and new entrants. Neither of these technologies leapfrogged what came before. Instead, their superior value to consumers was simply not widely appreciated at the moment of invention, and it took time for incumbents to realize it and adopt. Thus, the emergence of laser and MP3 technologies did not constitute disruptive events and (for the most part)[3] did not have disruptive consequences.

It is perhaps no coincidence that the popular knowledge of disruption emerged alongside the proliferation of the Internet. Digital technologies have fundamentally changed the economics of many industries, often removing inefficiencies and "fat." Whenever a new digital technology changes an existing service, especially when it significantly changes the underlying service itself, there is a temptation to draw the conclusion that the incumbents in the industry are being disrupted.

Is It Time for a Reeducation?

As I write this book, my own industry—education—is the target of a "disruption declaration." It began in 2011 when Stanford professors Peter Norvig and Sebastian Thrun decided to offer a course—*Introduction to Artificial Intelligence*—online and free of cost to anyone in the world.[4] 160,000 people enrolled for the experimental course, of whom 23,000 successfully completed it.[5] What is more, the top students all came from outside of Stanford and in some cases secured jobs as a result of their performance. Seeing the writing on the wall, Thrun promptly resigned from Stanford and launched the online education start-up Udacity. His intention was to continue offering massively open, online courses, a format that came to be known as MOOCs.

This example, alongside the innovations in K–12 education driven by the Khan Academy that have created tutorials and continual testing, caused many in higher education to worry that the jig was up. This was an industry where the "fat" that digital technologies could shed was plain to see. Higher education was suffering from a symptom of what economist William Baumol termed "cost disease."[6] This occurs when the wages of skilled labor in an industry are rising not because of more demand for the product of that labor, but because there is more demand for that labor as a result of productivity improvements elsewhere in the economy. Universities and colleges had moved to reduce the costs of that skilled labor: when professors lectured they spoke to ever-growing class sizes supplemented by smaller tutorials taught by adjuncts or graduate students. Furthermore, higher education institutions were employing more staff to extract funds in excess of tuition, such as through alumni fundraising, school sports, and research grants. This gave rise to an industry standard of higher administrative structures and costs and increased competition between institutions to raise the limited pool of funds (e.g., through new facilities, scouting trophy talent, running alumni events). Taken together, the higher education industry model that emerged caused tuition rates to rise faster than prices in other industries—in the United States, for example, tuition inflation has greatly exceeded general inflation rates.[7]

But what if digital technologies could hit the heart of the problem? What if digital technologies could allow colleges to scale the scarce resource—those famous professors—and relieve the burden of securing revenues from on-campus tuition or donations? The more elite universities and colleges acted fairly quickly (at least in college time) and within a few years were launching MOOCs of their own through platforms such as Coursera and iTunes U. Harvard and MIT got together and launched their own platform (called EdX).

At the same time, however, many within those institutions were concerned as to whether this would end well; MIT strategy professor Michael Cusumano, for example, worried that by offering free courses, elite institutions could drive out nonelite institutions and permanently damage their own brand, as "free" could be equated to "low-quality."[8] To my mind, while pricing your way back up from free can be a challenge, it is not a plausible alternative to simply dismiss an industry innovation like MOOCs because some incumbents have experimented with free delivery. Reversals in price and strategy can both occur, as evidenced by industry pioneer Udacity, which after only a few years of operation abandoned the "free" price in its own model of online delivery of education.[9]

Nonetheless, despite the press mentions and the millions of dollars that have been invested on these new experiments, MOOCs have yet to put a dent in the costs of higher education.[10] That is not to say that some of them won't eventually prove to be radical innovations and fundamentally alter the way students receive their education, but so far these prospects have not reduced demand for traditional education either, and there is speculation as to why. Many of my colleagues believe that online education is inherently inferior to traditional, in-class education; there is something about having to sit in a lecture hall that increases class completion rates.[11]

But when you think about it, the way we allocate resources for education is somewhat strange. So much effort is expended in producing locally grown products, which NYU's Clay Shirky described as the "artisanal" model pushed to its limits:

The minute you try to explain exactly why we do it this way, though, the setup starts to seem a little bizarre. What would it be like to teach at a university where you could only assign books you yourself had written? Where you could only ask your students to read journal articles written by your fellow faculty members? Ridiculous. Unimaginable.

Every college provides access to a huge collection of potential readings, and to a tiny collection of potential lectures. We ask students to read the best works we can find, whoever produced them and where, but we only ask them to listen to the best lecture a local employee can produce that morning. Sometimes you're at a place where the best lecture your professor can give is the best in the world. But mostly not. And the only thing that kept this system from seeming strange was that we've never had a good way of publishing lectures.[12]

Now one could argue that this "homegrown" model—repeated thousands of times—is a way of making sure the lecture material is kept up to date and at the frontier. But that argument, even as I write it, appears weak, as MOOCs have, as Shirky argues, demonstrated that many parts of education that we deliver as a bundle might be able to be unbundled.

The challenge MOOCs have laid down for higher education is that they look like they might be a disruptive innovation (their quality is inferior to the package of goods a college offers, but they might improve in some way to become a competitive threat). But they also hint that a new model of education would involve an architectural innovation. The components of that education might be the same, but how they are put together could be very different. Right at this moment, I, for one, cannot predict how this will all turn out. This is precisely the challenge incumbents and others have in predicting disruption.

This chapter will drill down into the prediction issue. Even though we know what disruptive events might look like theoretically—on both the demand and supply sides—it is less easy to identify them before the fact and disentangle them from nondisruptive technological inventions. If incumbents are going to manage their way through disruption—something that I address in the next chapter—it is useful to anticipate where it will come from. If entrants are going to bring innovations to market and attempt to replace the incumbents, they are going to want to assess their chances at success. After all, the flip side of the theory of disruption is that there are only opportunities for entrants when they can disrupt established firms. As I will demonstrate, it is far from obvious that such disruption, even when there is a clear opportunity for it, will be profitable for would-be disruptive entrepreneurs.

Can Disruptive Events Be Predicted?

There is a paradoxical sense in which, if disruptive events can be predicted, they cannot really be disruptive events. After all, if established firms knew for certain that an event could potentially lead to the failure of their business, then surely they would react. This suggests that uncertainty about disruptive events is an inherent facet of the phenomenon. Of course, both the demand- and supply-side theories give us some direction as to where to look, but can they actually do the job of predicting disruption?

Let's start with a reminder of the demand-side theory. According to that theory, disruptive innovations, from the perspective of established firms in an industry, do not satisfy the needs or desires of the existing customer base on key metrics, but they do manage to attract the unserved or the underserved. This is why these innovations initially tend to look like low-end products or products serving an unattractive new market. Eventually, however, they serve as springboards to more rapid rates of improvement on dimensions valued by existing customers of incumbents. Therefore, based on demand-side theory, we can only identify the innovation as a disruptive event as it improves rapidly over the current technology.

Herein lies the problem: there are many new products launched by entrants that target a niche and do not serve established firms' current customers. But only a few of these move on to the next step, achieving a trajectory of improvement that allows them to provide more value than current offerings and become a serious competitive threat. Put simply, you cannot actually disrupt an industry with a technology that most consumers do not like. It is only if the technology improves broadly, so that enough customers begin to switch, that the incumbents find themselves in trouble—facing disruption, according to the demand-side theory, that it may be too late to deal with.

This contradiction is part of the demand-side theory. It is easy to tell whether a technology is *potentially* disruptive, as it only has to satisfy the first step: it performs well on one dimension but not on the "standard" features of a given market. However, that is all you have to go on in making a prediction, because the second step can only be determined as events play out. If it were obvious that step 2 would occur, then everyone—entrants and incumbents—would see what the future might look like. In that situation, a potentially disruptive technology would not end up disrupting the establishment at all. Both incumbents and new entrants would have an equal shot of coming out on top: indeed, incumbents would have a better shot since they already have the customers. An integral part of the demand-side theory, therefore, is that we cannot know at the outset whether the second step in the process will occur or not.

Uncertainty and Dilemmas

That is what creates the "dilemma" in Christensen's *Innovator's Dilemma*. For an incumbent, it is costly to bet on a new, unproven technology when things are going fine with the old one. As an established firm, you could choose to react to everything that looks like it might be a disruptive innovation, but that would mean spending resources on many new products that turn out to be far afield from your own offerings. The reaction of higher education institutions to the potential MOOC threat is an example of this. Those institutions believed that online offerings were inferior to their current education delivery methods and experiences, but out of fear of being disrupted they invested millions of dollars in their own MOOC offerings. While it is not possible to say at this stage whether those efforts have been wasted, there is a concern that they are potentially just a marketing tool rather than a true educational tool. There may be very good reasons to experiment with online learning, but noting that MOOCs are inferior and then investing out of fear rather than a sense of opportunity does not suggest a carefully considered product design process.

This is an important point, so I want to emphasize it clearly here: *it is uncertainty over whether an event is, in fact, disruptive, that gives rise to the dilemma facing established firms.* Those firms have made a set of choices that have driven their success. In the demand-side theory, those choices have been customer-focused. In the supply-side theory, those choices have allowed more independence to teams devoted to improving components. The dilemma arises because, to face a disruptive threat, those prior choices have to be abandoned: a bad idea if it turns out that a potential threat is not disruptive, but a good one if the reverse is true. There are two propositions, or lemmas (in Greek), with associated actions whose worthiness is tied to the truth of a particular proposition. The dilemma becomes real when a particular innovation has appeared but there is uncertainty is to whether it is disruptive or not. As soon as the uncertainty is resolved, there is no more dilemma; there is a monolemma, if you will, or strictly speaking, just a lemma. There comes a time, then, where you know what the right course of action is—but at that point you may no longer have the chance to undertake the right course of action.

In the next chapter we will look at whether your choices to take actions in the face of events revealed to be disruptive are still available to you. For the moment, it is useful to see how uncertainty can be multifaceted. It is not simply whether an innovation might improve, but what might be the basis of that improvement.

To see this, note that it is implausible to assume even that an established firm can identify all the products that may turn out to be disruptive innovations. This is certainly an issue for higher education. All of the MOOC models pursued thus far put existing faculty—the so-called "scarce resource"—at their heart. One of the most successful MOOCs takes Michael Sandel's oversubscribed *Justice* course at Harvard and uses multiple cameras and professional editing inside one of Harvard's largest and oldest lecture theaters to make viewers feel like they are there.[13] The assumption is that the winners in the online education market will be the ones that bring the best in-class lecturing talent to the world. Even Clayton Christensen himself appeared in a similar production for the for-profit University of Phoenix.[14]

But what if that assumption is false? What if the star professors in the offline world are not the stars in the world of online education? In fact, we already have an inkling that this may be the case. While they may not be names in the halls of academia, CGP Grey, Vi Hart, Henry Reich, and Brady Haran have brought diverse explanations of mathematics, physics, political institutions, and history to millions on the Internet. Grey's videos, for example, regularly amass more than 4 million views.[15] And they are not Hollywood-level productions, just a carefully researched, scripted treatment using PowerPoint as the primary expository tool. None of these people have a research background, although a few have been teachers in the past. However, each of them has been able to delve into and assimilate academic knowledge to bring exposition to students. On the other hand, while many academics know a lot about their subject matter, it is not clear that they are experts in the exposition of this knowledge via online media.

Of course, coming up with better modules does not a disruption make. But then, as an academic I would say that, wouldn't I? My point is that no matter how widely an established firm may look to find would-be disruptive events, it will not be able to identify them all. Even established firms have limited resources and attention. Moreover, as the education example reminds us, we need to think about supply-side disruption. A university or college, in its most fundamental form, is a product whose components are delivered and improved upon using tried-and-true methods. What rarely changes is the way the components are put together. Online learning and the integration of technology in learning both represent potentially different ways of architecting the educational experience. Thus far, no dominant design for online education has emerged as it has for traditional educational delivery (e.g., lectures, assignments, and exams—it is quite amazing how a single model has proliferated around the world through some very different economic systems). Furthermore, it would be highly unlikely that a firm could experiment with a new architecture as that would require integrating significant changed throughout the organization. Given the uncertainty involved, predicting a disruptive new architecture seems pointless, because it cannot be acted upon. Therefore, both supply- and demand-side theories lead to the conclusion that predicting disruptive events is very challenging, if not impossible.

Is Prediction Worthwhile?

There are two poster children of disruption in photography: Polaroid and Kodak. Polaroid declared bankruptcy in 2001 and Kodak in 2012. In each case, the culprits were digital technologies and the changes they brought to the photography industry.[16] Also in each case, the firms saw the changes coming and invested heavily in the new technologies. In other words, this was a situation where the future was clear to established firms, yet that did not save them from failure.

Polaroid was the leading company in instant photography, by which a photo could be taken and developed right away, straight from the camera. As early as 1981, Polaroid saw digital technologies as a threat to its business and began extensive R&D into the new technologies. By 1989, 42 percent of its R&D budget was devoted to digital imaging. But according to research by Mary Tripsas and Giovanni Gavetti, Polaroid was never able to envisage what we know now as the right products to exploit those technologies.[17] Polaroid thought of itself as subsidizing cameras and making money on film. Thus, there was always a film element to its innovations. Management was also nervous about a change in competitive orientation.

As one senior manager noted, "We're not just going up against Kodak, Fuji, etc. We're going to be up against 30 consumer electronic companies—the Sonys, Toshibas, Hitachis, the Intels, etc. We need to have a unique idea that corresponds to our core capabilities and the way we relate to the marketplace." There was also concern about Polaroid's ability to simultaneously manage very different businesses as voiced by another senior manager: "Can we be a down and dirty manufacturer at the same time we're an innovator over here? Can you have two different philosophies running simultaneously in the company?"[18]

Had the camera been viewed as a stand-alone device, the trajectories Polaroid ended up pursuing might have been different. While it had a digital camera prototype in 1992, it only launched a product in 1996. Ironically, its digital image sensors led the world in resolution at the time, so it was well positioned for the digital camera business, but by the time it launched there were already 40 competitors and it was hard to stand out from the crowd.

In this account, Polaroid—while having clear predictions on the direction of technology—faced a classic, Henderson-Clark style of difficulty in reorganizing itself around what was essentially a new architecture. The message would seem to be that, when disruption is on the supply side, even perfect foresight is of limited use. For Kodak, by contrast, things appeared to be demand-oriented. In 1975, it was the dominant film and camera maker in the US. It was at that time, in fact, that it developed the first digital camera.[19] From that time, digital had always been on Kodak's radar. Indeed, during the 1990s it partnered with various information technology companies to produce digital cameras, for example Apple's QuickTake consumer digital camera in 1994. Kodak continued to be able to predict the market throughout the late 1990s: prior to 2000, the problem with a consumer digital camera was actually viewing the photos, as it was difficult to transfer them to computers. Once again, Kodak was on top of this issue, developing docks that allowed for easy sharing of digital images to PCs, allowing it to become the leader in the US market by 2005.[20]

Indeed, if there was ever a company in a position to defy demand-side disruption, it was Kodak—it was even one of the first few companies to consult with Clayton Christensen himself. Managers in Kodak read the *Innovator's Dilemma* upon its publication and used its messages to direct

Kodak's product strategy. One example of this was to launch cameras in toy stores as a defense against Nintendo, which had put them in one million Game Boys.[21] Nintendo's cameras were by all accounts awful, but they were enough to get Kodak worried about disruption.

Kodak was able to outpredict the market and to make substantial investments in what came to be disruptive innovations. Though they were initially inferior on multiple dimensions, they improved to take the market in less than a decade. Despite that, the company ultimately succumbed to the integration of cameras with mobile phones, which turned out to be the major consumer direction. Though leadership was aware of shift to digital technology, Kodak had not anticipated the need to add a mobile phone to its portfolio of technological improvements. As a testament to its ability to innovate in new technologies, in 2012, when it filed for bankruptcy protection, its most valuable assets were its digital patents, which sold to a group of its newer rivals for almost half a billion dollars.

Ultimately, Kodak illustrates that being on top of the phenomenon is simply not enough to save a firm from failure. Why it failed is open to debate. It certainly wasn't because it decided not to respond. Indeed, its investments in digital technology were as large as those of born-digital firms. But it could be that its hands were tied by history. For instance, Kodak invested heavily in hybrid products that would combine its existing strengths with the new technologies, for example the Photo CD, a way of taking film to photo shops and bringing a digital product home. The problem was that you still had to pay for film and development, the precise thing that a purely digital route would bypass. Kodak spent more than it ever had on R&D, only to see its share price obliterated.[22]

The notion that Kodak was bound by its history has been expounded by Brian Wu, Zhixi Wan, and Dan Levinthal,[23] who studied the company deeply. They argued that Kodak's key assets were a "prism" that gave it color blindness when it thought that color was its chief legacy. Large digital investments would only have been profitable if the end result was a restoration of Kodak's market leadership. As it turned out, for Kodak, whose strength was in film, digital photography would have meant inventing an entirely new company—and one that was not the market leader but just another competitor. In retrospect, perhaps its best and most profitable strategy would have been to fade gracefully. This should make us wonder whether an ability to predict disruption, even if it is possible, is of any value to established firms facing it.

Are There Industries That Are "Ripe for Disruption"?

We have seen that predicting disruption can be difficult because disruptive events tend to be multifaceted; even if you forecast some aspects of an event correctly, other aspects (including whether the event is driven by a disruptive versus an architectural innovation) can cause firms to slip up. Part of the ongoing business discussion about disruption has been the notion that some industries and some firms have more reason to be on their toes than others. Even if we cannot predict specific disruptive events, as these can only be identified after the fact, might it be reasonable to suppose that some industries are more "ripe for disruption" than others?

In popular discussions, industries singled out as being ripe for disruption are usually those that have noticeable inefficiencies. This is certainly true of education, but similar concerns have been raised in relation to health care, air travel, and, of course, taxis. The latter case has a regulatory origin—a restricted number of taxi licenses—that has removed competitive pressure in that industry. But when technological change allowed for the possibility of entry via some regulatory gray areas, startups like Uber and Lyft were able to swoop in and claim a share of the market.[24]

Indeed, it is often the case that technological changes themselves expose inefficiencies that suggest disruption is on the way. Advances in autonomous driving have suggested that road transport—both cars and trucks—may fundamentally change. But the potential applications of the technology are still hard to see. While Google has demonstrated the feasibility of driverless cars in normally trafficked urban areas, people may not trust their safety to autonomous vehicles when there are others around. Instead, it may be in less trafficked areas (neighborhoods or intercity highways) that autonomous vehicles find a disruptive niche. Or it may be that only a change in our thinking, to embrace sharing cars rather than owning them, will make autonomous vehicles the obvious technological path forward. It stands to reason that auto manufacturers are not turning a blind eye to all of these possibilities, because change seems so possible. Yet even assessing observed inefficiencies (relative to current technological possibilities) and determining disruption to be inevitable does not give firms much indication of its timing or nature.

Finally, I wish to dismiss one indicator of potential disruption that is so often referred to in public discussions: that a particular industry or firm will be subject to disruption because it is able to charge high margins. This is, of course, one of the reasons higher education has been targeted for potential disruption. However, the same charge is laid to banking, insurance, cable television, and many other sectors dominated by entrenched oligopolies or monopolies. These industries and firms cannot all be subject to disruption, because they are not making the same set of decisions that made them successful in the past. Such industries may now have inefficiencies or may underserve certain consumers, but the firms that grew to incumbency did not get that way by doing so. Instead, they took opportunities to compete with those that existed previously in order to establish a position in the market. For various reasons, they were able to acquire market power that insulated them from subsequent competition. That insulation meant that they could still be successful *without* having to do the things that made them so. They may have competed in the past, but in effect they competed for an annuity to have a relatively easy time of it in the future. Certainly such firms are still vulnerable to change and to failure, but in most of these cases new competition will have to be assisted by governments, either through direct regulation or through the application of antitrust laws. Though it does not rule out new sources of competition, this protection or "insulation" makes these incumbent firms very resilient.

A case in point is the typesetting industry that arranges words for printed materials. Typesetting, of course, dates back to Gutenberg and the invention of movable type in the 1400s. But, the modern approach of using a keyboard as a primary input device arrived in 1886 when Ottmar Mergenthaler invented the Linotype machine.[25] The approach used hot metal, pouring liquid metal to create the type. Until 1949, it was the only method of typesetting other than the much slower and more expensive letterpress, and Mergenthaler Linotype along with two other firms (Intertype and Monotype) dominated the entire industry. To say that this industry has undergone dramatic technological change is an understatement, yet to this day Mergenthaler remains among the dominant firms. How did this occur?

Mary Tripsas, who later studied disruption in photography, wrote her MIT PhD thesis to answer this question. She found the answer: fonts. In 1949, hot metal gave way to a photographic process using a xenon flash, then just over a decade later it was done digitally using a cathode ray tube, until finally laser typesetting arrived in 1976. In almost every case, previous competencies were made redundant by a new technology and established firms struggled to produce leading machines for the next generation. It was a classic issue associated with the reinvention of architectural knowledge, yet in each case these were not disruptive innovations. The new entrants' products technically outperformed the incumbents', but it was only in the move from hot metal to photography that those entrants made significant market inroads—and even in that case, an incumbent (Intertype) was actually the first to market.

The problem new entrants faced was that they were missing one thing—what David Teece terms a *key complementary asset*.[26] Without that asset, entrants could not compete with established firms. The primary customers of typesetters were newspapers and publishers. Each had a look and feel to its products that depended crucially on the font it chose. As it turned out, the vast majority of fonts were proprietary and owned by the incumbent hot-metal typesetters of which Mergenthaler was a pioneering leader. In the late nineteenth century, it aggressively invested in developing new fonts, building a library of 100 typefaces by the turn of the century (which grew tenfold just a decade later). 500 typefaces was considered a minimum number to be viable, and, at Mergenthaler's aggressive rate, an entrant would need five years of continual development just to be competitive.[27] It simply did not matter what type of machine was being used to implement it; if a customer wanted Helvetica (a Mergenthaler font which is the most famous font of all time), it would have to purchase from Mergenthaler. Mergenthaler did not own any specific intellectual property other than the trademark on the name, but that still proved enough to give it an advantage. The dominant technology for the machines may have changed over the years, but the fonts never died. This meant that incumbent firms could take their time in adopting new technologies and restructure their organizations accordingly, because their customers were loyal to their chosen fonts.

This experience should again make us hesitate to identify industries that are ripe for disruption. Even in situations where the criteria and processes for disruption turn out to have been met, other factors can protect incumbents. One suspects that this is why the modern textbook industry—where books can retail at $100 to $200 or more—has not been subject to the large changes that ordinary bookselling has. Put simply, the customers (educators, and subsequently their students) have invested in familiarizing themselves with and structuring their courses around certain textbooks, making it difficult for new entrants to dislodge them. Similarly, the TI-84 graphic calculator has survived for over a decade and is still priced above $100 (when a $0.99 app can do the same thing) and sells in the millions.[28] Why? Because teachers have invested in knowing how to use it in class and exams, and the producer, Texas

Instruments, knows that. Sometimes firms can hold market power while continuing to do the same things that made them successful because there is a particular factor (such as a key complementary asset) that makes it hard for them to be dislodged. At the very least, market power is something that can give a firm breathing room to formulate an appropriate reaction to what would otherwise be disruption.

Uncertainty Is Endemic

Prediction is useful if it can be turned into actions that matter. This chapter has suggested that there are two reasons why the activity of prediction may not be ideal in the face of disruption. First, disruptive events can come from many sources, and even if you are convinced that, say, digital technology will change your industry, it may not be obvious *how* it will do so. Second, one of the reasons prediction is difficult is that a particular disruptive event may not, in fact, undermine the fundamental competitive advantage of your business in terms of the possession of key complementary assets.

These uncertainties pervade the current choices being made in higher education. Many investments are being undertaken in order to keep educational institutions on top of digital technologies and to preemptively establish footholds among what might be competitive threats that arise from them. But at the same time, it is far from clear that these will, in fact, be the source of disruptive events. For instance, MOOCs may not be the way in which digital technologies fundamentally change the way we deliver education. Moreover, they may not change some of the key complementary assets held by higher education institutions, in terms of how to put together educational resources and to keep them relevant and useful over the long term.

That said, uncertainty generates opportunity as well as fear. The opportunity comes from being able to consider the managerial options for dealing with potential disruption. As when facing the impact of a new disease, there are two broad approaches here: going for a cure or going for prevention. The advantage of going for a cure is that you can manage uncertainty after it is resolved. This prevents you from allocating resources to false starts and dead ends. The alternative is trying to get yourself into a situation where you can prevent the disease from impacting you. In the context of uncertainty, that is akin to taking out insurance before the fact and hoping that it shields you from whatever comes. Much of the discussion regarding disruption has, in fact, focused on the latter. It has pushed managers to fear disruption and to find opportunities before the fact that allow them to rest easy. These will be addressed in chapters 6 and 7. Before that, however, I want to explore a restless path that involves the options for dealing with disruption after the fact. Whether a manager chooses to manage disruption before or after it occurs, spending brain cycles trying to predict the precise path a disruptive event may follow is something that can be set aside.

5

Managing Disruption

Perhaps one of the reasons disruption has been so widely discussed in the media is that many people believe media industries themselves are going through it. This is particularly true of newspapers, which have made a transition to a digital world in terms of what they do but not in terms of their business model. The diagnoses for what ails the newspaper industry range far and wide. Digitization and the advent of services like Craigslist have caused them to lose the classifieds business (which went from being like printing gold to not being worth the paper it was printed on). Newspapers now cope with a flood of competition for reader attention from blogs, independent outlets, national and global news outlets, and, of course, social media. But most critically of all, advertising revenues have diminished as readers have moved online. In the US, total advertising revenue (nonclassified) for newspapers today is at about 40 percent of where a forecast made in 2000 would have predicted it to be.[1] It is hardly surprising, then, that after a decade and a half newspaper people lament "[c]an't we just get finished being disrupted already and get on with our lives?"[2] Whether it is truly disruption or not (as defined by our terms in this book), it is hard to argue that the Internet has been anything other than disruptive to the newspaper business in the dictionary sense of the word.

In this context, we got a rare insight into how businesses were using the phenomenon of disruption to manage issues they were facing. In March 2014, an internal (but glossy) report entitled *Innovation* leaked online.[3] It was the outcome of a task force within the *New York Times* designed to outline the challenges the *Times* was facing and to prepare staff for a raft of organizational changes designed to meet them. The essential challenge was clear: "We have always cared about the reach and impact of our work, but we haven't done enough to crack that code in the digital era." The *Times* had falling readership numbers, with 1.25

million print subscribers and 760,000 digital subscribers.[4] Those numbers were healthy by industry standards, but they were not enough to support the journalistic endeavors of the *Times* as they had in the past. Put simply, it was far from clear that, in economic terms, any of the news the *Times* was supplying was still "fit to print."

There are two interesting things about this document. The first is the diagnosis of the problems facing the *Times*. Put simply, the company claims it is facing demand-side disruption. The second is the list of recommendations it proposed to manage the problem. These recommendations are the focus of this chapter: if you are facing disruption, what can you do to manage its impact from this point on? I will consider in detail the report's recommendations, but first it is useful to consider and evaluate its diagnosis.

In a chapter entitled "Disruption: A Quick Overview of the Competitive Landscape" the report outlines Clayton Christensen's theory of demand-side disruption. It recognizes that disruptive innovations are introduced by industry entrants, sold at a lower price point than existing products, target an underserved or new market, are advanced by an enabling technology, and are initially inferior to existing products in the market. In the report, those entrants are the digital-first outlets like the *Huffington Post* and *BuzzFeed* which are taken to be of lower quality (although I have to say that depends on how you view your customer), cheaper (e.g., free to readers), and do not target traditional *Times* readers (at least initially). They are enabled by the Internet but also by social media distribution as a means of pulling readers to their outlets. The report notes that those outlets are now moving upstream and the quality differential between themselves and the *Times* is getting blurred. In other words, they are now a competitive threat.

The *Times* worries that, while it can rest on its laurels and believe that its customers are different, it may also risk becoming Kodak.[5] Hence, it wants to alter what it is doing internally to position itself to compete head to head for the customers the new entrants have already managed to attract. Interestingly, as we will discuss further, while many of these ideas actually move the *Times* organization toward mimicking the new digital entrants, its past still looms large.

Not a single person among the hundreds we interviewed ever suggested tinkering with the journalistic values and integrity that make the Times the greatest journalistic institution in the world. But we must evolve, and quickly, to maintain that status over the coming decades.[6]

The report never quite grapples with what "evolve" means, and an external reader, such as myself, could surely be forgiven for thinking the *Times* is trying to have its cake and eat it to. It is the tension between both preserving what has made an organization great and incorporating new competitive changes that lies at the heart of managing disruption.

The Shadow of Replacement

How should an established firm react to a potentially disruptive new entrant? There are actually two important forces holding the established firm back from any immediate reaction: uncertainty and the cost of reaction. First, consider *uncertainty*. As discussed in the previous chapter, there is a real probability that the entrant's product will fail to become a competitive threat. From both the demand and supply sides, the product may never rise to the minimum quality necessary to threaten the established firm or be able to be supplied in a sustainable, profitable manner by the entrant. Either way, the threat may be dissipated without action from the established firm.

Second, any competitive reaction is likely to be *costly*. This occurs for reasons of simple logic: if the actions comprising a reaction were profitable for the established firm to do when no entrant was pursuing the innovation, it would already be doing them. If it is only because of new entrants that it becomes sensible for the established firm to consider an innovation, the reaction must incur costs (relative to when there was nothing to react to). For this reason, we should expect established firms to be reluctant to react to prospective competition and maybe even to some actual competition.

Consequently, there is a sense in which an established firm, by moving to meet an entrant, will always be initially sacrificing some profits from its existing business. There are no free lunches here, only tradeoffs. We can see precisely what those tradeoffs might be at an operational level. If the *Times* could just have introduced digital products without an impact on its traditional print business, this would have been an easy decision and would likely have occurred, regardless of competitive pressures. The problem is that digital products cannibalize some existing print sales. That does not sound like a bad tradeoff until you realize that the print business is subject to economies of scale. In particular, each customer that falls off the route of a distributor of the printed newspaper is a pure loss of revenue for the newspaper. With new competitive pressures in the digital realm, *Times* management recognizes that at some point the print business may become unviable. Thus, by adopting digital products, the *Times* is accelerating any inevitable decline in the print business, while trying to stay relevant on the latest news technology trajectory.

This notion—that established firms face a dilemma in introducing new products or innovations because this cannibalizes their existing, profitable businesses—has been a core part of economic analyses of innovation for half a century. The theory, termed "the replacement effect," was investigated by Nobel prize winner Kenneth Arrow in a highly influential publication in 1962.[7] To understand it, consider what it would mean for an incumbent to adopt a new innovation. If it adopts, then the new product will replace the incumbent's existing products, and customers will move away from the existing products to the new one. Thus, the value of early adoption is the difference between the profits a firm receives from the new product and those it would have received from the old. By contrast, an entrant has no existing products and no "baggage"; its net benefits from adoption are not reduced by the presence of existing profits. Consequently, when it comes to incentives to adopt the new technology, an entrant has stronger incentives than an incumbent, precisely because the incumbent has an additional concern—the cannibalization of its existing profits. To put it another way, incumbents have diminished incentives to hasten the decline of their current products, whereas entrants have no such concerns.

This suggests that incumbents may generally have diminished incentives to innovate, so as to reduce "competition with themselves." In reality, this only applies to certain types of innovations. For example, while Microsoft in the 1990s might have had reduced incentives to produce operating systems for products other than personal computers (as every sale of an alternative would reduce its sales of Windows), the same was not true for upgrades of Windows or add-on innovations such as web browsers or media players. In this situation, Microsoft was incentivized to enhance Windows so it could generate new sales and expand its market. This example illustrates that not all innovations create tensions for incumbents.

A Competencies Perspective

Should we think of cannibalization and replacement as purely related to the products a firm sells and the profits they generate? Academics Michael Tushman and Philip Anderson believed the matter went deeper than that.

They saw that a firm's existing profits depended not solely on its products but, perhaps more importantly, on its competencies. Competencies are the skills, abilities, and knowledge that a firm possesses: in modern parlance, the "soft" or intangible stuff. In research published in 1986, Tushman and Anderson classified major technological changes as either competency-enhancing or competency-destroying.[8] Sometimes a competency-destroying innovation was something that created a new product class (like xerographic copying machines or the automobile); in other situations, it might involve innovations to a process of production. For instance, for glass manufacturing, float-glass processes could do what continuous grinding and polishing did, but with better quality and lower cost. The final product that the customer saw was the same, but the skill set required to produce it was fundamentally changed.

Tushman and Anderson were not so much interested in whether firms failed but in where the innovations were coming from: from incumbents or entrants. Their study of twentieth-century airline manufacturing, cement production, and minicomputers in the US largely confirmed their prediction that, when it came to major technological discontinuities, ones that enhanced the competencies of incumbents would be initially adopted by them while those that destroyed incumbent competencies would initially be adopted by new entrants.

Looking at competencies has a natural compatibility with the broad theory of the replacement effect. Innovations that enhance an incumbent's competencies can both be more easily adopted and also allow the incumbent to capture more value from its existing products. By contrast, those that destroy an incumbent's competencies would put it on a more level playing field with new entrants in terms of the costs to bring the innovation to market—as all firms would have to develop new competencies—but, as per the replacement effect, would diminish its incentives to do so.

Seen in this light, the replacement effect (or its Tushman-Anderson variant) is an important element of the theory of disruption. A disruptive event arises when there is a new product opportunity in a market. The demand-side theory focuses on the costs incumbents face in adding that new product today: the costs of integration, brand confusion, or a loss in focus. The supply-side theory concentrates on the incumbent's costs of reorganization needed to generate the knowledge necessary to meet the new opportunity. Taken together, all of these factors might reduce the profits the incumbent could otherwise achieve. Add the fact that the incumbent's existing customers, at least in the short run, may not prefer the new innovation, and the incumbent would see an immediate loss in sales. This means that the incumbent would have little incentive to absorb the costs of adopting an innovation.

The replacement effect can also be seen as a future concern. An incumbent could adopt a disruptive innovation today so that it can control the innovation as it improves along all product dimensions. But even if doing so involved no displaced profits today (say, because the incumbent found a way to manage an independent "firm within a firm"), the incumbent would still have a diminished incentive to innovate as this would accelerate the obsolescence of its existing products. The more rapidly an innovation improves, the faster the profits from an incumbent's existing products are dissipated—resulting in little incentive for the incumbent to invest in adopting an innovation.

Consequently, the replacement effect is a key part of disruption theory.[9] In addition to the effects on existing profits, an incumbent firm must also consider the degree of market power (or lack of competition) it might face. The relationship with market power is a subtle one. Holmes, Levine, and Schmitz argue that incumbent firms often have switchover costs associated with adopting new technologies.[10] These costs mean that the immediate impact of such adoption is higher marginal costs and a corresponding loss of sales even if, in the future, that impact is overcome. Clearly, the higher is a firm's margin on its current sales (a proxy for its market power), the more costly is the switchover. Thus, increased current market power (and not simply a large market share) can be a disincentive to adopt new innovations. The replacement effect and uncertainty are two reasons why an established firm will be reluctant to react to new-entrant innovations even if these might precipitate a disruptive event.

Doubling Down

The iPhone represented a new entry into the mobile handset industry. While incumbent handset makers discounted the iPhone's attractiveness both to consumers and to carriers, Apple had been so successful with the iPod that they knew they had to respond. Apple had signed an exclusive arrangement with AT&T in 2007, an arrangement the leading carrier Verizon had declined.[11] Following the reaction to the iPhone's new design, Verizon, in particular, was desperate to ensure that it had a competing offering. It approached many, but the challenge was first taken up by RIM.[12]

One reaction to disruptive events is for incumbents to raise their game on their own products. This is a natural consequence of competition. Indeed, this is one of the reasons why entry on the basis of disruptive technologies can be so effective. Precisely because it appeals to a niche set of customers initially, entrants can fly under the radar of incumbents and avoid a response. With the iPhone, Apple was hardly moving under the radar. Steve Jobs was motivated by the notion that smart phones were not that smart, they didn't have the full Internet, they certainly didn't have a music player, and that the keyboard took up half of the phone's surface area where, often, other stuff could reside. He specifically faulted the BlackBerry and claimed that Apple's new phone would capture one percent of the market within a year (amounting to 10 million phones sold). In other words, Apple was inviting reaction.

While publicly dismissing the iPhone, RIM did indeed react. When RIM's founder Mike Lazaridis opened the iPhone, he saw that it had a Mac inside and that mobile computing could well be the future.[13] Only a couple of months after the iPhone's launch, Lazaridis pitched a new device to Verizon and the European company Vodafone. The BlackBerry Storm had the heart of a BlackBerry but the large touch screen of an iPhone. Lazaridis had heard Jobs's critique of the physical keyboard and responded. As the BlackBerry keyboard already used predictive tools to ensure that users could type well in a small space, coming up with an on-screen touch keyboard was not difficult. What was more, Lazaridis believed that people wanted a tactile response when using a keyboard. The iPhone didn't provide that, but when you typed in the Storm, the whole screen clicked in response. The carriers embraced the new device.

It took over a year for the prototype to reach the market. By then Apple had released a second iPhone, this time worldwide and with 3G capabilities. Nonetheless, armed with a $100 million marketing blitz, the Storm was an immediate hit, with one million sold in the first two months.[14] But there was a problem. To pull off this feat, RIM had rushed the development of the Storm. While BlackBerries had a reputation for durability and ensuring that everything worked, the Storm fell short. Lazaridis had told his engineers that he had "to fix everything that's wrong with the iPhone,"[15] but he hadn't done so, and in the process had broken everything that was right with the BlackBerry.

The reviews were scathing. David Pogue wrote in the *New York Times* that "[w]hen you look at your typing, slow and typo-ridden, and you repair the dents you've made banging your head against the wall, you'll be grateful that Verizon offers a 30-day return period."[16] And return them they did. Verizon reported that virtually all of the million Storms sold needed replacing.[17] This would cost Verizon half a billion dollars, and it wanted RIM to pay. RIM held its ground and offered some reimbursement, but the whole episode had harmed its relationship with its best customer. In doing so it started a process that would cause carriers to embrace Android as the alternative to Apple. More critically, the episode had delayed by two years any real response by RIM to Apple.

When entry is not disruptive in our sense of the word (i.e., doesn't lead to the failure of incumbent firms), doubling down on a firm's existing strengths can be an effective response. It can allow firms to leverage what they have—in RIM's case an email solution and user-friendly device—while ensuring that the entrant is contained. The problem arises when entry is disruptive. In this case, a response can be attempted, but if it doesn't work out as people expected—in this case, carriers and customers were caught off guard despite initial enthusiasm—it can accelerate a firm's troubles. This is what makes disruption such a difficult event for great companies.

Wait and Double Up

Sometimes when an existing organization is threatened, it doubles down on its historic strengths, reinvesting in them in hopes of warding off a threat. RIM did this with the Storm, keeping its historic strengths while meeting just one flaw in its offerings—the small screen. By contrast, we could use "doubling up" to describe a situation in which an existing organization meets a threat by changing its focus and investing in new areas at an accelerated rate. Disruption theory tells us, at a minimum, that doubling down may be a bad idea. By contrast, the replacement effect suggests that "doubling up" is a hard thing to do. However, as time goes on and the nature and reality of a disruptive event are realized, the returns to doubling up increase significantly.

To see this, consider a situation in which an established firm is convinced that a new entrant has an innovation that will threaten it competitively. In this situation, there is no future in which the firm can keep doing what it is doing and be free of competition. That competition is inevitable, and hence replacement is already taking place. In this situation, the established firm is now on an equal footing with the new entrant in terms of their incentives to introduce the new product. This is the situation the *Times* now finds itself in. It has assessed that new entrants will now be gaining ground with the paper's own customers unless it adopts the technologies—digital, social media, and the like—that the entrants have been using. Hence, its response is to try to replicate the new entrants' approaches to digital news production and distribution. You can see this in the *Times* report's recommendations: to focus on audience development (e.g., moving from page one to things like social media to find readers), to bring technology into the newsroom by having it more integrated with the business side that is focused on reader experience, to embed a strategy team inside the newsroom to create linkages and digital experiments, and finally to be a digital-first organization. Each of these is an investment to make the product of the *Times* more similar to those of its newest rather than its traditional competitors.

In contrast, throughout the report the *Times* also senses that it has an advantage precisely because its traditional customer base is still loyal. That is, it sees an opportunity to adopt the new digital tools but to keep a relatively exclusive hold over its traditional base. For this reason, the report does not challenge the notion that the *Times* should be investing in the production of quality journalism that its traditional base values. From that perspective, the investment equation for the *Times* becomes different from that of new entrants. Economists Richard Gilbert and David Newbery explained in 1981 that when an established firm can defend a monopoly segment against innovative entry through investment, its incentive to protect its monopoly will be greater than the incentive for new entrants to invade.[18] The established firm is the only one that can maintain monopoly-type profits, while new entrants can hope at best to profit through competition with the incumbent. Monopoly profits are typically larger than competitive profits. It is easy to see that monopoly trumps competition as a prize any day.[19] Thus, if the *Times* believes it can defend its traditional base against the competition, it will be incentivized to double up its investment in the new technology in an effort to retain its monopoly-type profits.[20]

What causes a firm to switch from being constrained by the replacement effect to being motivated to double up? For the *Times*, what has changed is that dragging its feet can no longer prevent the entrants from competing. Previously, the digital options were insufficient to threaten the paper's traditional base, perhaps due to the lack of convenient mobile connected devices. Now it cannot slow that competition down; its future is no longer determined just by its own actions but rather by those of the new entrants. Thus it makes sense to double up to defend its most profitable existing areas from that competition. Action rather than inaction becomes the best defense.

While it is hard to know whether the *Times* will actually succeed in this, we can look to history in other industries to see whether doubling up has been a successful response. Intel held off AMD, which at various points innovated faster and further than Intel in microprocessors. Intel did so at the cost of a manyfold-greater R&D budget and by holding onto distribution channels in ways that eventually raised the ire of anti-trust authorities.[21] Critically, Intel's assets of its brand and distribution channels were still useful in the face of new microprocessor configurations. It should be noted, however, that those advantages can also diminish. As I write this, Intel faces strong challenges from smaller mobile chipsets (think tablets and mobile phones) that do not need to fit inside computers.

Microsoft, the "Browser Wars," and Doubling Up

Perhaps a more direct example of doubling up comes from an interesting recent study by Rebecca Henderson along with Tim Bresnahan and Shane Greenstein. They considered the challenge faced by Microsoft upon the arrival of Netscape, the first real web browser, and with it the personal Internet. Netscape was of concern because it threatened to provide a challenge to the Windows operating system. To be sure, the challenge was far from immediate and also far from obvious to consumers. However, to Microsoft's leadership, it was a very real threat and required immediate action.

In the mid to late 1990s, Microsoft initiated the "browser wars" with its own weapon against Netscape, Internet Explorer.[22] However, it did this by setting up a separate and well-resourced division within Microsoft, separate from the extremely successful (at the time) Windows division. Windows had its own approach to the Internet through the Microsoft Network (MSN) that would control the user experience on the Internet and also the services it would direct consumers toward. (A similar approach had been pursued by AOL.) In other words, Microsoft hoped to guide consumers to applications that complemented its existing Windows/MSN ecosystem.

It is not entirely clear why Netscape gained traction before Microsoft had a chance to respond. One might suppose it was below Microsoft's radar, in the manner of a classic demand-side disruptive event; but Microsoft had consistently monitored developments in the Internet space, so it was aware of what was happening there. Instead, Microsoft's initial reaction looks more like a classic replacement effect story. In

1994, Microsoft CEO and founder Bill Gates still pushed proprietary services as the only profitable way to bring the Internet to consumers. By 1995, with Netscape taking off commercially and also launching interfaces with online applications that mimicked Microsoft's own approach with Windows, the danger was clear to all: Netscape could own a key complement to Windows that would not be under the control of Microsoft.

Microsoft dramatically changed course. Gates penned an eight-page memo outlining the threat, making Netscape the exception to the "avoiding the costs of integration" rule.[23] It threw resources at the problem, launching successive versions of Internet Explorer in an attempt to take share from Netscape. There were challenges, as Netscape was pursuing an open-systems approach (with its browser available across computing platforms) whereas Microsoft had traditionally not competed in this way. Microsoft's organizational capabilities were mismatched for this challenge, and realignment of the existing organizational divisions would take time. For these reasons, Microsoft had to invest in creating an entirely new division. This was no small division; it had 4,500 people working for it. While Gates still oversaw its strategic direction, it was largely autonomous and completely focused on catching Netscape. By 1998, it had done so, but it had not done it quite alone. The new division had drawn upon many assets that were used elsewhere in the organization, particularly in marketing and the PC distribution channel. This was not without cost, as some concessions were required in order to get its browser installed by equipment manufacturers. Moreover, Microsoft had to make a strategic choice to allow this new Internet Explorer division to render much of MSN irrelevant.

The doubling up on the browser had put Microsoft in a position to beat Netscape and perhaps dominate that segment for a long time.[24] But it is perhaps instructive that, when it achieved that position, Microsoft no longer assessed its legacy businesses as being in peril. It had more control over its destiny. Not surprisingly, this meant that the independence of the Internet division that had allowed victory in the browser wars became itself an issue. The tension peaked as the Internet Explorer division wanted the browser to be available for all users of Windows—even legacy users—while the Windows division wanted Internet Explorer's new features to be available only to those who purchased the latest version of Windows. This also manifested itself when Microsoft tried to do a deal with AOL for Internet Explorer to be offered to all AOL subscribers. AOL wanted, in return, visibility to users of Internet Explorer. For Microsoft's MSN, this represented a clear, competitive conflict.

As Bresnahan, Greenstein, and Henderson document, the conflicts that emerged became resolved in a very traditional way: the Windows division took control of the Internet Explorer division. While this likely preserved extremely high profit streams for the company for some more years, it is harder to see whether this was the right decision for the long term. Certainly, over the last decade, Microsoft has faced continual issues in terms of managing its legacy businesses alongside new opportunities. Then again, while its star may have dimmed, Microsoft, unlike the old mobile handset makers, is still strong in a number of areas; including its traditional strengths. From that perspective, one wonders whether the dramatic "browser war" reorientation was worth it.

The case of Microsoft illustrates that, when it comes to launching new products under the same banner, firms face "diseconomies of scope." These arise for a simple reason: at some point, those products will draw upon *shared resources* and thus are never truly independent. Because of this, internal debates will arise, and it may be hard to make the case that the new division should continue its independent run once its initial mission is complete.

The Microsoft case suggests that it is possible to manage disruption by doubling up. What is also true is that this requires significant resources to be marshalled and expended, likely much more than if these firms had been able to manage the competition prior to the disruptive event and the growth of new entrants. It does suggest that missing a disruptive event does not inevitably lead to failure. Instead, managers whose firms have the right capabilities can draw on them to respond competitively. I leave to chapter 7 a discussion of precisely what those "right" capabilities are.

Wait and Buy Up

When faced with a potentially disruptive event, waiting allows an established firm to learn and possibly reassess whether that event is truly disruptive and then take action. Matching a competitor's efforts is what doubling up is all about. But another path is to coop the competition through acquiring the competitor. Moreover, acquisition is a particularly powerful solution as a reaction to disruption, as it avoids the need to pay for developing products to compete with the myriad of potentially disruptive entrants and to integrate those entrants' products and technologies into the incumbent's own mainline business. However, the longer an established firm waits to see if a new entrant is actually disruptive and has the potential to wipe out the established firm, the higher the cost of acquiring a new entrant is likely to be. Indeed, in some cases, as we saw with Netflix and Blockbuster, waiting too long may mean that there is no price that could lead to an acquisition.

Acquisition allows an established firm to neutralize the disruptive threat, sometimes completely. This does not mean the innovation is necessarily lost, but instead that the established firm has time to adjust and has control over how the innovation is adopted and integrated with its other products. In other words, the established firm can manage the replacement effect. Thus, we would expect to see a pattern of an established firm waiting to see whether an entrant is a potential threat and then cooperating with it in some manner.

In my own research with coauthors Matt Marx and David Hsu, we examined more than 50 years of start-up strategies in the automatic speech recognition (ASR) industry to see what patterns were associated with disruptive innovations.[25] It has been a long-standing goal to enable computers to understand human speech. Recently we have seen this technology embedded in our mobile devices (e.g., Siri, Google, and Cortana), but previously it was deployed in more pedestrian settings including, most notably and often most frustratingly, call centers. This industry had a mix of established firms but also many entrants that brought innovations into the industry. As it turns out, hundreds of firms have brought innovations into the market, slowly but surely improving speech recognition. Each time, there was also considerable uncertainty about the new technology's prospects.[26]

Our focus was not on the performance of the established firms. Instead, we looked at disruption from the perspective of entrants. Our hypothesis was that if an innovation was sustaining rather than disruptive, then an entrant would be more likely to do some kind of cooperative deal (e.g., licensing, an alliance, or an acquisition) with an established firm. Indeed, in our data, entrants were 60 percent more likely to cooperate with an incumbent initially if they had a sustaining rather than a disruptive technology.

Had we stopped there, this would have looked consistent with demand-side disruption, perhaps to the lasting detriment of established firms. Instead, however, we looked to see whether entrants persisted in their strategy or pivoted to some other choice later on. A well-known example is Siri, a speech-recognition-based "personal assistant" that was initially launched as an independent app before it was acquired by Apple in 2010.

These patterns have been part of the history of the industry. A lesser-known but earlier start-up called Vlingo Corporation integrated speech recognition in a mobile app with a disruptive innovation based on grammar-free speech recognition.[27] This was a technology that did not confine users to a set of recognizable phrases, like existing technologies at the time, but allowed them to speak freely. Not surprisingly, it was less accurate than previous technologies, but the accuracy improved over time. On a mobile phone this allowed users to dictate text messages rather than simply identify someone to call. Vlingo's long-term goal was to embed its technology in mobile handsets with a licensing deal. However, because of poor performance on traditional metrics, it needed to prove that consumers would accept these tradeoffs by going to the market itself through a mobile app. This strategy worked, and Vlingo was later able to secure licensing deals.[28]

In effect, Vlingo switched from competing with mobile handset providers to cooperating with them. It wasn't alone in switching its strategy. We found (controlling for other factors) that entrants with a disruptive technology who started out competing with incumbents were four times more likely to make this same switch to cooperation as those with a sustaining technology.[29] What this suggests is that incumbents can wait and then cooperate with the most promising entrants as a strategy to manage disruption, particularly demand-side disruption. This makes intuitive sense, as it is precisely when those technologies have proven themselves to generate performance increases on traditional metrics that they become a threat to established firms. So long as there aren't any other barriers to cooperation, this is a valuable option for established firms. Moreover, while they may pay more for such cooperation when a disruptive technology becomes proven, they save on the costs of reacting to or acquiring nascent startups that do not pan out as successful disruptive innovations.

Managing Demand- versus Supply-Side Disruption

Thus far, I have presented the wait-and-double-up and wait-and-buy-up options for managing disruption reactively, without making a clear distinction between demand- and supply-side disruption. This was because in many cases disruptive innovations have architectural elements, and vice versa. Nonetheless, it is important to note that the management options presented here may work more effectively for demand-side than for supply-side disruption.

Recall that the value of waiting before acting lies in the fact that it can take some time to resolve uncertainty as to whether a disruptive innovation is on a trajectory that will competitively threaten an established firm. Prior to that point, the replacement effect suggests that it is optimal for a market leader to slow rather than speed up the adoption of innovations. For demand-side disruption, the threat emerges when an entrant with a disruptive innovation starts to make inroads into the established firm's main product markets and to take away its mainline customers—specifically, the customers who had earlier said they were not interested in the disruptive innovation. When this is the case, the established firm can adopt the disruptive innovation via investment or acquisition and take more control over how the industry is changing. In particular, it can take steps that will allow it to have an impactful competitive role in the future. It will face conflicts in thinking about how to achieve that, given short-term conflicts with its existing business, but for a purely demand-side disruptive event it will be able to adopt the new innovation.

Supply-side disruption theory, in contrast, makes us question whether waiting and then acting can be a cure for this form of disruption, as dealing with this form requires absorbing new architectural knowledge. The problem faced by established firms is not the acquisition of such knowledge but instead the integration of different ways of doing things into an organization that already has ingrained processes. Doubling up and acquisition do not allow an established firm to magically absorb architectural knowledge; incumbents must invest in the costly process of integrating that knowledge into their organization. For that reason, in such a case it is hard, for instance, to find a price an entrant might accept for a cooperative deal. And by the time the wait-and-see strategy makes it clear that an incumbent might wish to acquire an entrant, the entrant has a commanding bargaining position. In either case, the entrant could obtain a solid market position without the assistance of the incumbent. This explains why wait-and-see can itself be a costly tactic for incumbents, and why a successful acquisition cannot be guaranteed.

That said, a firm could potentially prepare itself for the integration challenges associated with reactive doubling up or acquisition in the face of supply-side disruption by proactively gaining capabilities for such integration. This is something we return to in chapter 8.

Wait and Give Up

We have already seen how Kodak anticipated many of the innovations in digital photography that would later be the cause of its demise. In many respects, Kodak pursued a doubling-up strategy on those new technologies, including investing heavily in hybrid products that would combine its existing strengths with the new technologies. Given the largely architectural changes required of its business model and the competencies this destroyed, one wonders whether, in retrospect, perhaps Kodak's best and most profitable strategy would have been to fade gracefully.

This is easier said than done. How do you know when to just give up in the face of technological change? After all, I have argued that there are ways of managing disruption, and there is uncertainty regarding how things will play out. There is no simple answer here, but in at least one instance I found a company that was able to just say no.

In 2009, I purchased a Flip HD camcorder. Around the same time, Cisco purchased Flip, the company, for about $600 million. It was never clear what Cisco was up to, but with YouTube being a big deal at the time, combining Internet connectivity and digital video creation seemed like an obvious synergy. It took Cisco just a year to change its mind, announcing in April of 2010 that it would shut Flip down.[30] Cisco's move sparked surprise and even outrage. Flip had 500-odd employees, was earning $400 million in revenues, and had grown 15 percent the previous year.[31]

But even those opposed to the shutdown understood the problem. For example, mere months after its purchase I sold my Flip on eBay for about half of what I paid for it to an elementary school teacher who wanted to let his students make movies: I never had it with me and it was too complicated to just pick up and quickly shoot whatever my kids happened to be doing. My new toy, an iPhone 4, could do the same job more easily and I always had it with me. That story hung over the product category like the sword of Damocles. But Flip's fans seemed outraged that Cisco was not going to try harder to keep Flip a going concern.

In comparison with Kodak, Cisco's decision to cut and run on Flip was unusually visionary. Why not do it now rather than sink many hundreds of millions more trying to hold on, while stringing customers along to make network investments on their videos? While Flip's competitors in pocketable camcorders plough on, time has shown that Cisco likely made the right call.[32]

It's All in the Timing

This chapter has shown that managers have options when faced with what are clearly disruptive events. But one thing to stress about those options is that they create what financial economists term *option value*. When a new technology arises, over time it becomes gradually clearer whether it will prove to be a disruptive event and in what way. Thus, by waiting, a firm can obtain information that assists it in making better decisions later on. In other words, prior to making a choice, keeping your options open has value.

Timing, however, is an issue. Suppose an entrant comes into the market based on a new innovation and that it is possible for an established firm to meet the entrant head on. Specifically, while there are challenges on the supply side in doing this, for demand-side disruption the premise is that there are no constraints in deciding to meet the competition, although there may be costs in terms of not satisfying the firm's long-standing customers. Under this assumption, the established firm faces a decision regarding how intensely to meet the competition, whether quickly and aggressively or slowly and cautiously. The advantage of reacting quickly and aggressively is that this may provide a competitive response to the entrant that puts the entrant's own plans and even viability in question. For the established firm, this provides a possibility of retaining its market leadership.

The disadvantage of this, and the advantage of a more cautious approach, is that the quick reaction accelerates the inevitable. That may not matter if the inevitable is just around the corner, but what if it is some years away? Consider, for instance, how long it took for the Internet to develop news media sites that actually challenged the incumbent newspapers as news sources: at least a decade and, by some markers, far longer. Indeed, the digitization of news was a forecast associated with increased computer proliferation way back in the 1980s. Even today, while the *Times* is feeling competitive pressure, there may be many more years left for its traditional approach. Thus, if the *Times* were to act quickly in becoming more like the digital entrants, it might end up pushing away its traditional customers quickly and losing a steady stream of profits as a result.

This is where the *Times'* strategy to deal with disruption has some apparent issues. Almost all of the *Innovation* report's recommendations involve doing something differently within the paper's internal organization. The *Times* already has digital products and offerings like its competitors. The issue is that those offerings are not gaining traction with consumers outside of the paper's traditional customer base and even within some segments of the existing base. It could be that it has not doubled up appropriately and slipped the shackles of the replacement effect. But it could also be that what *BuzzFeed*, *Huffington Post*, and other smaller organizations do is something different internally. Without a legacy organization or, indeed, certain procedures for journalism, those sites' teams are organized differently, perhaps with far less centralized editorial oversight and certainly with much more technology devolved into the hands of content creators. If this is the case, then the *Times* will find it hard to pursue a strategy of evolving a new organization from its current one.

The point is that the *Times* has chosen this as the time to exercise its option to do something quite radical with its internal organization. I have no special insight into whether the timing is appropriate. However, from the perspective of someone who has spent years studying the changes taking place in the news media as a consequence of the Internet, it is still far from obvious what the disruption really is and how it can be managed. The *Times* is treating the disruption as coming from a distinct product, but the issues may equally be tied to changes in the advertising market that have little to do with specific products. In taking actions at this time, the *Times* is placing a bet regarding the future. Moreover, it is doing so in a way that it has not done before, something we will discuss in more detail in the following chapter.

6

Self-Disruption

In January 2010, Steve Jobs did it again: he announced the iPad, a device that would finally move tablet computing forward.[1] Countless others had seen a tablet as a natural computing device after it was featured as a tool in *Star Trek: The Next Generation*. A start-up, GO, and then Microsoft had each spent hundreds of millions to develop a tablet-style computing solution.[2] But Apple decided that its dominant design for smart phones would, literally, scale up to a tablet-sized device. This time around, the debate centered on whether Apple was cannibalizing its own computer business with this tablet.[3] Apple, it turns out, didn't care; but RIM became worried that with the iPad, Apple might make inroads into RIM's growing and successful enterprise business.

Mindful of the failure of the Storm, RIM decided that this time it would do things differently. Mike Lazaridis cracked open his copy of *The Innovator's Dilemma* and decided to follow its prescription.[4] Instead of taxing and refocusing the engineering divisions that were generating new BlackBerries, he would set up an autonomous group to develop RIM's response to the iPad, the PlayBook. He realized that this new device would have to be built from the ground up, including a new software system that was not based on the outmoded Java one that powered existing BlackBerries. In particular, he needed an operating system that could handle a web browser with touch capabilities. "We embraced [*The Innovator's Dilemma*] and did our best to reinvent the company. Everything would have to change."[5]

The PlayBook was developed according to the self-disruption play-book:[6] to survive disruptive innovation, established firms needed to set up autonomous business units to take charge of meeting disruptive innovation. While we can wonder, with the benefit of hindsight, whether the iPad was truly disruptive to RIM, RIM's leaders saw that possibility. They believed that if iPads became used for corporate interactions, it would be a short step before enterprises adopted iPhones as well. The RIM leadership embraced Christensen's prescription that the firm's mainstream business would be oriented toward its current customers, so that a new unit was needed that would not care about the mainstream business. In other words, RIM had decided that it needed to disrupt itself.

Christensen considers self-disruption using autonomous business units to be the only way to deal with demand-side disruption. While we noted in the previous chapter that doubling up or acquiring entrants could also save a firm from disruption, those actions are costly. In each case, they involve difficult decisions as to how to allocate resources and meet disruptive threats. Some firms, of course, may have capabilities that make these reactions easier—for instance, Microsoft had marshalled resources to meet competitive threats many times in its history, and acquisition was a persistent feature in the voice recognition industry.[7] But in other cases, those capabilities may not be present.

Especially before disruptive innovations reveal themselves, Christensen argued that autonomy was the way to avoid the conflicts and dilemmas that disruption exposed while at the same time allowing the firm to respond in a way that matched the entrants' freedom to innovate and develop new ideas. "Companies can create new prioritization criteria, or values, only by setting up new business units with new cost structures."[8] The idea was that, like entrants, these new units could make decisions without regard to the impact on resources, business models, or margins of the main business units.

What does *autonomous* mean? Our research suggests that geographical separation from the core business is not a critical dimension of autonomy. Nor is ownership structure. There is no reason why a disruptive venture cannot be wholly owned by its parent. The key dimensions of autonomy relate to processes and values. The disruptive business needs to have the freedom to create new processes and to build a unique cost structure in order to be profitable as it makes and sells even its earliest products.[9]

Here, then, was a solution that was in the power of CEOs. Take resources and silo them to meet the disruptive threat. There was no need to spin off divisions or locate them far away from the head office.

This chapter explores the idea of self-disruption as a way of preempting disruption itself, particularly demand-side disruption. The proponents of supply-side disruption did not favor autonomy as a response precisely because new architectural knowledge required bringing the organization's units and teams together and creating new linkages. For that reason, I focus here on self-disruption as a response to demand-side disruption only, leaving to the next chapter the discussion of the equivalent preemptive response to supply-side disruption.

It should also be emphasized that self-disruption does not involve long-term innovation divisions (another managerial tool centered on autonomy). Google has created a separate and independent arm called GoogleX that is devoted to what it terms "moonshot ideas."[10] These ideas have included such things as Google Glass, autonomous vehicles, and, more recently, drone delivery, balloon-powered wireless Internet, and using data to increase human longevity. These are projects that face a different commercial issue than ones designed to disrupt existing businesses: these involve no disruptive threat but require a decision calculus so long-term that the usual methods of internal decision making are not suited to them. Consequently, they are siloed to make it possible to explore riskier projects.

Pure Self-Disruption

In coming up with the solution of setting up independent divisions to deal with disruption, Christensen was motivated by the case of Quantum Corporation—a hard disk drive manufacturer in the 1980s and 1990s. That firm was a significant producer in the 8-inch hard disk drive segment (which served minicomputers)[11] but did not achieve the same status in 5.25-inch drives (which served personal computers). At the height of its first success in 1984, some engineers within Quantum saw the potential for 3.5-inch drives, including a growing market, the personal computer. Quantum financed a new venture (Plus Corporation) as a separate entity but retained 80 percent ownership of it. According to Christensen, Plus operated successfully as an independent corporation and established a market presence in 3.5-inch drives, leading that market by 1989. Prior to that, with sales of its 8-inch hard drives waning, Quantum acquired the final 20 percent of Plus and adopted Plus's management and organization as its own. It continued as a significant producer from that time until its hard disk business was acquired by Maxtor in 2001. What Christensen saw in the Quantum experience was a path by which a firm could manage disruption. To be clear, Quantum had already been subject to disruption as it was focused on selling drives to minicomputer manufacturers (as opposed to the mainframe computers which were its initial market), but by setting up an independent entity to explore other customer segments, Quantum was able to revive itself in a new form at a later time and avoid failure. Christensen himself was unsure whether to regard Quantum as the same firm over the course of its shift from its minicomputer to personal computer orientation.[12] To Quantum's shareholders, however, the decision by managers to allocate capital to the new, independent venture appeared to be quite prescient.

What Quantum did by setting up an independent division actually has a long history in business. Lockheed Martin set up a division (Lockheed Advanced Development Projects) during World War II as a way of accelerating the development of jet engines.[13] Over the next few decades, it gained a reputation as a fast and secret division that developed all manner of new innovations in aviation, including the famous U-2 spy plane. The facility ended up being called the "Skunk Works" because of its existence (i.e., its "smell") and its secrecy, a play on the "Skonk Works" factory in the 1940s comic strip *Li'l Abner*. For our purposes, a skunk works is an independent division of a firm set up and owned by the firm but with a distinct mission to explore new technologies free of goals, presumptions, and the culture of the firm itself.

Theoretically, it is easy to see why the notion of a skunk works is appealing as a means of preempting demand-side disruption. When a potentially disruptive technology comes along, a successful firm will rationally shy away from putting resources into it because of resource dependence and simple uncertainty. To exploit a new technology requires a development process in the same manner as a new entrant might employ, without challenges and frictions. Thus, there is a hope that an established firm can create an entrant within itself through an independent division.

Skunkworks, however, are extremely challenging to execute. As Christensen emphasized, such a division really has to be independent—a spinout akin to Plus Corporation:

How separate does the effort need to be? The primary requirement is that the project cannot be forced to compete with projects in the mainstream organization for resources. Because values are the criteria by which prioritization decisions are made, projects that are inconsistent with a company's mainstream values will naturally be accorded lowest priority. Whether the independent organization is physically separate is less important than is its independence from the normal resource allocation process.[14]

This was easier said than done. Christensen envisaged that the CEO of the established firm would have to ensure that the resources and capital allocated to the autonomous unit were shielded from other pressures. This would require some active defense. Furthermore, as it was the most successful established firms that faced the innovator's dilemma, this required a strength and enlightenment that not many CEOs would possess.

Then What?

The experience of Quantum Computing represents a pure form of self-disruption—that is, setting up an autonomous unit that is on top of the disruptive event and stands ready to be the company once the mainline business is disrupted. Surely we need to question whether such a pure form is really a good thing for an established firm. After all, if it has assets, resources, and capabilities in its mainline business, those will all be destroyed, whether the disruption is carried out by an autonomous unit or a new entrant. Shareholders could have achieved the same return by investing in the established company or in the new entrant. In this regard, self-disruption looks like delegating to a single company the job of diversified portfolio management.

Such delegation may in fact be efficient: if the established firm's resources can be useful in developing a new disruptive innovation, then its managers may have an advantage in identifying and efficiently allocating those resources to the new venture. While this is a sound hypothesis, I will point out that it is at odds with the main concern regarding disruption—that established firm managers and organizational choices are at a disadvantage in allocating resources to disruptive threats. While there are some business leaders who can perhaps cut through that paradox, as an investment strategy this does not seem to be a general principle people can rely on.

Instead, surely the reason to self-disrupt is to give established firms the *option* of managing the process and specifics of disruption down the track. As we noted when discussing Microsoft's experience with a separate Internet Explorer division in the late 1990s, an independent division may develop innovations and then, because it is owned by the established firm, be integrated back into that firm in a way that might allow for the coordinated management of both old and new assets. At the very least, losses from competition between the new and old could be mitigated, but there may also be opportunities to preserve valuable parts of the old business in the newer environment. Once again, however, an owned but independent division need not be the means by which this occurs. As we noted in chapter 5, an established firm could effectively treat new entrants as autonomous units with an option to acquire them. The difference here would be a reduction in the frictions in achieving that outcome, with a tradeoff between the speculative investments associated with a spin-out or autonomous division and the potential premium the established firm would have to pay to acquire an entrant later on.

The Self-Disruptor's Dilemma

The charge of independence is to bring the advantages of a start-up dynamic into established firms. But can this truly occur? To be sure, if the mainline business dies regardless of the activities of the autonomous unit, then that unit can become the main business. However, what if the mainline business's main competitive threat becomes the autonomous unit? In many respects, that is the point of self-disruption—to disrupt your own business *before* others can do so. But unlike an entrant, the autonomous unit faces a commitment problem: *it is owned by the established firm, and that firm, by dint of its ownership and control, always has the option to rein in that division.* Thus, if the purpose of the autonomous unit was to resolve the innovator's dilemma—that is, the inability of a firm to turn away from its own customers' preferences in favor of the disruptive innovation—then the self-disruptor's dilemma is that this very same dilemma does not go away. There comes a point where the established firm has to decide whether to keep disrupting itself. And that involves precisely the same tradeoffs as the innovator's dilemma.

This reformulated dilemma is perhaps best illustrated by IBM's response to the personal computer (PC). IBM was the first great computer company to offer a platform to enterprises. Up until the 1980s, it dominated enterprise computing with its mainframes, most notably the System/360. It offered a vertically integrated solution that took sales and support into the hearts of firms and then a system design that allowed for modular development of components.[15] But even the System/360, introduced in 1964, was not without internal controversy. "It was a multimillion-dollar gamble for the firm, opposed by all existing computer product line managers."[16] This move required IBM to adopt a new organizational form that put sales and support front and center, making IBM a customer-focused company. That, however, meant that when it was time to compete with the new minicomputer architecture, IBM stumbled and ceded the minicomputer ground to others.

The minicomputer lesson turned out to be valuable when the time came to consider the PC market. The early leader in that market was Apple; in the late 1970s, IBM found its own enterprise customers purchasing Apple II computers in order to use the revolutionary VisiCalc spreadsheet program and word processors. This time, IBM was prepared. By then it had realized the need to monitor new architectures; as Bresnahan, Greenstein, and Henderson document, it had a group based in Boca Raton that was charged with monitoring small-system developments. That group, apparently in a single presentation to IBM senior management by Bill Lowe, convinced the firm to make a significant PC investment.[17] They assessed, correctly as it turned out, that PCs were a disruptive event.

This was not an obvious insight at the time, and there was really no competitive pressure on IBM to enter that market. But enter it did, and did so moreover with a separate division, enabling it to insure against demand-side disruption. The goal was to ensure that the PC standard would not be controlled by others (e.g., Apple) and that IBM could continue an enterprise push. In stark contrast to IBM's vertically integrated and proprietary approach, the PC division pursued an open-system approach. For IBM, that meant relying on components that were external to the firm to ensure that they were the best for the new architecture, instead of using its usual internal, integrated procurement.[18] The openness also necessitated transparency that eschewed IBM's traditional approach of consulting its best customers. Given all this, the only way IBM could proceed was to allocate resources to an independent business unit. The Boca Raton group were actively shielded by senior management against corporate pressures that might have challenged what they were doing.

As Bresnahan, Greenstein, and Henderson describe, there was virtually nothing about the PC division that adhered to the norms, practices, and procedures that IBM had pursued so successfully elsewhere. For example,

Boca Raton—in keeping with its mission to "act like an entrant"—also did not depend on IBM's own distribution network, instead arranging for distribution through third-party retailers, Sears and Computerland. This brought the IBM PC into a distribution mode suitable for the individual end user, rather than the corporate computer department which was closely linked to the IBM field sales force.[19]

It is hard to imagine a choice going more against the core of IBM's sales-driven culture at the time. Indeed, the PC division felt the weight of history early on. As it tried to implement its third-party development of the operating system and applications, it struggled with distrust from potential vendors due to IBM's protection of proprietary assets elsewhere. This hindered the PC division's ability to work the best vendors and instead forced it to consider less conventional choices such as Microsoft.

As it turned out, the PC division was spectacularly successful in its entry, and the IBM PC became iconic for a couple of decades. This success, however, was in many ways fleeting. Utilizing IBM's open standards, clone PC makers entered strongly and soon surpassed IBM in technical competence.[20] Proprietary standards also eventually emerged—including later Windows and the 086 microprocessor architecture—but they weren't controlled by IBM. So how was it that a company that had seemed to do everything right did not end up with a large share of the rewards?

The answer lies in the fact that *pure* independence was a pipe dream. There are shared resources at the heart of many large, successful firms, and competition for those resources gives rise to conflicts. For IBM's PC division, the main issues arose around reputation. Personal computers were a new industry going through a period of experimentation and learning. Inevitably some projects did not work out (e.g., the ill-fated PCjr targeting home users), and the bad press from those false starts impacted beyond IBM's PC division. IBM's "reputation for reliability" was a shared resource and therefore had to be managed. This was also true of sales channels. As the PC began to have an enterprise impact, its separate sales channel came into conflict with IBM's Sales Division. These conflicts filtered into many parts of the organization:

By 1984, the PC Division had revenues of more than four billion dollars—making it the third-largest computer company in the world, had it been a stand-alone company. The issue arose because a significant fraction of that revenue was not contributing to sales commissions. Both the Sales Division and Sears could sell PCs; the internal IBM divisions received the PCs at a discount. The large accounts were held by the Sales Division, but the smaller firms and independent buyers could purchase from Sears. Thus, IBM had an internal division competing with an external company for the sales of its product. A complex set of rules determined who could make a sale, who would get credit (and commissions) for a sale and so on.[21]

So even apart from concerns such as the replacement effect, using a separate division to compete for the same customers could not be easily coordinated. Add to that the notion that for the PC division a "sale was a sale," whereas for the mainframe division a sale was part of a relationship: the philosophies were completely at odds with one another. IBM subsequently chose to reintegrate the PC division five years after it was formed, and the division proceeded to lose all of its early advantages in that market. Thus, it is fair to say that IBM just did not go far enough. The corporation faced real coordination issues with respect to the PC and other divisions. Bresnahan, Greenstein, and Henderson concluded that the issues were intractable:

> The IBM example illustrates the critical role of organizational scope diseconomies in fostering misalignment. It was ultimately impossible for the firm to manage both the PC business and its existing large-system business within the same organization. Conflicts arose over the deployment of fundamental strategic assets, IBM's reputation as a firm and its relationship to its corporate customers. The conflicts were fundamental. ... Where the open-systems PC business called for quick, "good enough" new products compatible with PC-market competition and innovation, the existing proprietary large-system business needed predictable product upgrades, compatibility in connection between large-systems and small-systems, and high reliability. There was no resolving the conflict.[22]

To my mind, the seeds of IBM's failure in PCs were sown when it chose an autonomous approach to the PC. It was this response, aimed at preventing future disruption, that undermined the firm's ability to nest self-disruption within itself so as to deal with demand-side changes. In other words, the innovator's dilemma was not resolved by IBM but merely delayed. In the end, while it kick-started the PC business, the sustainable businesses from that market were handed to others.

Self-Disrupting and Knowing It

The great microprocessor business Intel had its origins at the opposite side of the computer, starting in 1968 as a memory chip business. The memory business had been extremely successful, as Intel pioneered a process of putting metal on silicon so that it could increase the number of circuits in a chip at a lower and lower production cost. Its design became dominant, which invited intense competition. Thus, through the 1970s Intel's profit margins began to fall. This gave rise to internal conflicts. The development scientists were still motivated to bring about larger, more revolutionary changes, while the manufacturing engineers wanted more reliability in the production process.

Robert Burgelman documented the increasing tensions at Intel.[23] Its technical scientists were developing new memory chip generations that to the marketing department only had niche applications. Intel's market position started to erode. But in the midst of all this, Intel won a contract to supply a new chip to a calculator manufacturer. One technical scientist, Ted Hoff, saw that the chip could evolve into a new architecture—the microprocessor (a new type of microchip that allowed complex functions to be performed). He convinced upper management that such microprocessors, if developed, could generate more sales for memory chips. This entree allowed a new competence in implementing design architectures in logic to emerge especially around understanding complexity as opposed to chip density. Thus, the microprocessor turned Intel away from process innovation and toward product innovation.

What Burgelman argued was that the top management of Intel were unaware of this fundamental change in their company. Their corporate strategy still considered memory chips as a core technology in the company, and they did not understand how important the personal computer was going to become. Here was Andy Grove (Intel's chief operating officer at the time):

Don't ask managers, What is your strategy? Look at what they do! Because people will pretend. ... The fact is that we had become a non-factor in DRAMs [dynamic random access memory], with 2–3% market share. The DRAM business just passed us by! Yet, many people were still holding to the "self-evident truth" that Intel was a memory company. One of the toughest challenges is to make people see that these self-evident truths are no longer true. ... I recall going to see Gordon [Moore] and asking him what a new management would do if we were replaced. The answer was clear: Get out of DRAMs. So, I suggested to Gordon that we go through the revolving door, come back in, and just do it ourselves.[24]

For middle managers all of this was frustrating, but fortunately for them they were empowered to pursue opportunities as they saw them. Consequently, those responsible for microprocessors were able to continue to move quickly and develop those markets, even if they had to compete at a high level for major capital resources with the memory business. By the mid-1980s, top management finally understood the change and the company made important exits from the memory business.

Intel's experience is that of a company dealing with disruptive-scale change. It was fortunate for them that middle managers had sufficient autonomy to be able to seize on, exploit, and develop a new opportunity that became the company's primary focus. While it was unplanned, the effect was akin to the ideal of self-disruption. But it also highlights the challenges of the self-disruptor's dilemma. It took many years for Intel to realize that its own business had changed, and that it could capitalize on this in a way that led to market dominance for decades thereafter. But the problem with the self-disruptor's dilemma is that the same choices can so easily go the other way.

Message Not Received

Consider, again, the experience of RIM. Four years after the iPhone was introduced, RIM was still growing, with revenues in 2011 up 33 percent over the previous year. This was driven by sales outside North America.[25] In the rest of the world, BlackBerry's bandwidth economization remained a key feature, while even its older models remained a cheap option for many users. What drove those consumer sales was not the BlackBerry's use for email but instead an app—BlackBerry Messenger or BBM. With 50 million users in 2011, it was, by far, the first global killer app for mobile phones.[26]

BBM was born the same way as Intel's microprocessor business: deep inside the company. In 2003, a trio—Chris Wormald, Gary Klassen, and Craig Dunk—investigated how to translate popular instant messaging services (like Yahoo, AOL, and MSN) to the BlackBerry. The idea was to allow for real-time text messaging. The critical feature was to give users a way of knowing whether a message had been delivered and read. Users of the instant messaging services loved how they knew what the status of a message was.

For something that would become so successful, management at RIM were dismissive for some years. "Back at RIM, not everyone was enamored of the BBM trio spending so much time on a self-directed pursuit outside of their duties."[27] "Klassen's boss would shoo Wormald away if he saw him in the building, scolding him for distracting Klassen from his duties; and he gave Klassen a bad performance review—for spending time creating BBM."[28]

Here is the self-disruptor's dilemma asserting itself again. Firms have limited resources, so that even if employees see opportunities, management may react against them. Nonetheless, the trio persisted, and BBM was launched and became an immediate hit.

In a world where the iPhone and Android did not exist, BBM would have helped BlackBerry secure an advantage for its product. But with those phones able to have independent apps developed, messengers soon appeared for them. An app like WhatsApp (which was bought by Facebook in 2014 for an estimated $19 billion)[29] was cross-platform, which by 2011 gave them access to a much larger set of users than BlackBerry. For RIM, as BBM was driving its handset sales, it kept BBM for Black-Berry only.

The debate regarding what to do with BBM started at RIM's top management. Senior product manager Aaron Brown argued to co-CEO

Jim Balsillie that BBM should be opened up.[30] Sure, RIM might lose handset sales, but there was evidence of decline there anyway. He saw that the firm could be reinvented around this software product, gaining and building on critical network effects. He also believed that this model would allow RIM to coopt carriers into the plan with a subscription model designed to stem its losses in SMS revenues. Balsillie was convinced and made it a strategic priority.

At this point, the board asserted control on strategic direction. It hired Monitor Group to report on various options. Monitor called for RIM to focus on its handset sales, believing that opening up BBM would bring only modest returns.[31] The board backed the Monitor approach. There would be no change in the business, and a few months later RIM's founding co-CEOs were effectively out of the company.

History now tells us that there was considerable value in mobile instant messaging. In 2011, BBM led the messaging market, and it would not have taken much for it to have capitalized on that. But this idea—that the future of mobile data communication lay more in software and hardware—was disruptive, and at the time it was hard to objectively see that value. The mobile app market was still in its infancy, and the idea that messaging apps could be worth more than RIM itself would have struck many as laughable. In the end, the only way messaging could reach its potential was outside of established firms. Self-disruption's elements were there, but the will finally wasn't.

Can You Pick Disruptive Winners?

This chapter began with the PlayBook, RIM's response to the iPad built on the model of self-disruption and autonomy, with RIM co-CEO Lazaridis taking charge of the operation. RIM's new device would discard the operating system inside BlackBerries and build on a new one, QNX, that RIM had acquired.[32] Moreover, it would address weaknesses with the iPad, including the lack of a camera and a port to link to high-definition televisions. It would also include Adobe's Flash that Apple had chosen not to support on its devices but for which there existed a large developer community. And, finally, RIM would move quickly, aiming to release its device just six months after the iPad.

In the process of doing all this, the PlayBook team made what would have been an unthinkable decision for the main organization: it decided to ship the first version of PlayBook without an email app. On the one hand, that was the point of an autonomous self-disrupting team: it would make unthinkable decisions. On the other hand, when the PlayBook appeared without an email app, the market was confused. To be sure, you could read email on PlayBook, but you needed a BlackBerry and it was awkward. And without this feature, was it really a device aimed at enterprise customers? Even the name "PlayBook" seemed to detract from that positioning.

The PlayBook failed for RIM, and it had to write off its costs only a short time later.[33] In retrospect, it is easy to see that poor decisions were made, but also that the very autonomy championed as the self-disruption path prevented checks and balances from the main organization from pushing the PlayBook toward a product that made sense for BlackBerry. To be sure, autonomy is designed precisely to free a unit from an organization's normal checks and conflict points. But those checks may be there for a reason; in RIM's case they were.

This demonstrates the real challenge associated with disruption. Even if it operates along the designed path, it may not block outside disruptive elements. It presumes there is only one or a few potentially disruptive technologies that could be developed by independent divisions. In reality, the uncertainty that surrounds disruption means that it may not be possible for a successful firm or its own independent skunk works to identify and develop all of the potentially disruptive threats. In other cases, including for RIM, it may identify threats that turn out not to be threats. In that respect, the self-disruption approach might seem more like a lottery than a means of reducing the risks of disruption.

7

Insuring against Disruption

Thus far, we have shown that established firms may be subject to disruption that could cause them to fail, and that by managing disruption, either by acquiring entrants or by doubling up to meet the new threats, they can prevent this failure. But in each of these cases, it is perhaps critical to have capabilities that make management of disruption effective, or to have key complementary assets that allow you to buy time for an effective response. Acquisition requires being able to integrate the new entrants into your operations to supply products on new technological trajectories. Doubling up requires marshalling resources to build a competitive response to new entrants. This can be costly, especially if disruption involves architectural innovations that require not just launching new products but a reorganization of internal product development practices.

Managing disruption involves reacting to disruption and dealing with it after it has emerged and any uncertainty has been peeled away. But what if you want to insure your firm against disruption before disruptive events arise? Firms may desire to fortify themselves against any disruption, or more reasonably to be in a position to ride out any disruptive storm. Is there such a thing as *proactive* management of disruption?

In theory, self-disruption is, in fact, a means of being proactive, at least about demand-side disruption. However, as demonstrated in the previous chapter, it is rare that all issues can be resolved by pursuing independence. In particular, a firm will have to integrate the independent unit at some point, just as it might have had to do with a new entrant. And this is in the best-case scenario in which self-disruption has chosen the right innovations to pursue.

In this chapter I will argue that, in fact, if a firm wants to insure against disruption, the mindset it should adopt is the opposite of independence: *integration*. This is the approach that was recommended by Henderson,

Clark, and others who developed the theory of supply-side disruption. The idea is that in order to deal with new architectural innovations, firms need to continually challenge themselves to understand the linkages in their organization and evolve them to meet and assimilate innovations that emerge. Integration has been shown to be an effective proactive strategy to deal with what otherwise might have been disruption. Moreover, even though it was designed to target supply-side threats, integration also allows firms to develop capabilities to more effectively manage all disruptive threats after the fact—both demand- and supply-side. That said, while integration does provide insurance, there is clearly a premium to be paid. To proactively use integration to prevent disruption often involves sacrificing short-term competitiveness and even market leadership. Thus, real dilemmas are introduced for the firm in terms of trading off profitability and sustainability.

A Primer on Insurance

When we think about insurance, we often think about unpredictable events such as fires. Your house might burn down for a myriad of reasons, and therefore you want to take out a policy that will transfer back to you the money you need to rebuild or to buy a new house. For instance, if your house burnt down you might receive $250,000, and you assess the probability of that occurring in a given year as one in 1,000. Then a fair premium to pay for a year of insurance would be $250, and if you were risk-averse you would be willing to pay even more than that. Things are a little trickier when you think about life insurance. In that situation, the probability that you will eventually die is one hundred percent. But when you buy a year's worth of life insurance, what is relevant is the probability that you might die during that year. Unlike with a fire, however, the probability that you might die is increasing each year, which means that a fair premium will be rising as well. That does not mean it isn't worthwhile to take out life insurance when you are old, but it does mean you would be giving up a large amount of money that might otherwise be spent on fun activities.

Insuring against disruption is more like life insurance than fire insurance: the premiums go up over time because, if you believe disruption theory, the longer you are successful, the more vulnerable you are to disruption. The actual situation for firms is even more challenging as there is no actual insurance company that offers a policy on disruption. Instead, by insurance we mean making preemptive investments and commitments that can reduce the probability of disruption. The problem is that the size of the asset (the firm's value) that you are trying to protect rises over time and the cost of taking protective actions increases in proportion to that value. As we will see, this implies that starting early in proactive management is desirable but at the same time risky, because you are placing a bet on future success.

Before turning to those actions, it is worth considering why an entrepreneurial insurance company does not offer actual "disruption insurance" to firms or their shareholders. We can also imagine a scenario in which shareholders are able to create their own "insurance." For instance, had shareholders in Kodak worried about disruption from digitization, they could have insured against this risk by buying shares in cell phone manufacturers. Problem is, that move is only obvious in hindsight; if you were an investor in the early 1990s, consider the options you had as hedges against Kodak's potential disruption: Nokia faced its own disruptive threat, Apple and Samsung were stagnant, and Google had not been formed yet. The very uncertainty that plagues management of disruption also makes it very difficult for shareholders to diversify in ways that mitigate the specific risk. Hence there are no purely financial options available.

Failure to Align

The notion of integration as a way to ride out waves of disruption arose from a study Rebecca Henderson conducted to earn her Harvard PhD. From 1987 to 1988 she immersed herself in the photolithographic alignment industry.[1] This industry demonstrated that supply-side disruption could be a recurring and important phenomenon. However, while the industry's market leaders were often displaced as a result of disruptive events, one company, Canon, was able to operate as a significant producer through successive generational changes in technology. Working out how it achieved this allowed Henderson to develop the theory of how integration could operate as a defense against disruption.

While many technology industries are relatively easy to understand, photolithographic alignment is a hard one even for those of us who consume research like this on a daily basis. It is highly technical and also holds an obscure position in the value chain. Photolithographic aligners are used in the production of semiconductors (like microprocessors). You may have seen the production of these as chips on a wafer of silicon: the patterns that make up the chips are printed using a process called lithography, and aligners are used in the printing process to ensure that the right pattern is transferred to the wafer. Importantly, by improving the alignment phase, you can print smaller features, improve yield (percentage of wafers successfully produced), and also increase the number of wafers a given aligner can handle. In other words, better aligners are not a new product innovation that final consumers will care about per se, but rather a new process innovation that can produce the same thing more efficiently.

Recall that the supply-side theory of disruption looks to see whether architectural innovations are associated with successful-firm failure. Thus, we need to know which innovations were architectural and which were not, and which firms were entrants at the time innovations appeared and which were established incumbents or market leaders. Henderson and Clark argue that, while there was continual incremental innovation in photolithographic aligners, there were five separate waves or generations of architectural innovation (table 7.1 summarizes those waves).[2] To argue that these were architectural innovations requires a careful study of the technology to understand how these innovations changed the critical relationships between components rather than the components per se. To reach this conclusion, Henderson conducted hundreds of interviews with engineers across the entire market.[3]

Table 7.1 also lists the market leaders at the time each innovation was introduced as well as the firms that introduced the innovation. The latter were all entrants to the industry, and in each case the entrant moved to become a market leader in the generation of technology it introduced. The reason this may constitute supply-side disruption is that, in each case, Henderson found that the price (adjusted for the quality) of the aligning equipment was not impacted by shifts between these

Table 7.1
Architectural Innovations in Photolithographic Alignment

Equipment	Date	Leading Incumbents	Innovating Firms
Contact aligner	1965	Kulicke and Soffa	Cobilt
Proximity aligner	1974	Cobilt, Kasper	Canon
Scanning projection	1974	Canon, Kasper	Perkin-Elmer
First-generation stepper	1978	Perkin-Elmer, Canon	GCA
Second-generation stepper	1982	GCA, Perkin-Elmer, Canon, Kasper	Nikon

generations. If these were improvements on characteristics (e.g., resolution quality) that were valued by the dominating customer groups, they would be priced at a premium over the previous generation, but that was not the case for these process-based technical innovations.

But if these technology generations did not have a demand-side impact, what clues are there that they are driven by supply? Henderson found that the incumbents and entrants had very different R&D allocations. The incumbents spent much more than entrants did for R&D on incremental innovations (60 percent more) but about the same as entrants for architectural innovations. This behavior manifested itself in the evolution of market shares between incumbents and entrants for the new generation. Put simply, the entrants, on average, obtained more than half the market in their first year of entry. By contrast, when an incumbent was the first to introduce a product based on a new architecture, it only gained 7 percent of the market in the same period. Moreover, incumbents with more experience in previous generations of the technology fared *worse* in terms of the amount of market share gained per dollar of R&D spent on new architectural innovations.

While the data indicates that supply-side disruption was at work, Henderson's in-depth interviews in the industry identified the mechanism for disruption as the inability of market leaders to absorb new architectural knowledge. For instance, in just five years Kasper Instruments had grown to supply half the market with a contact aligner. In 1973, Kasper realized that a proximity capability could improve its product and decided to introduce it. Microprocessor manufacturers, however, did not widely adopt the proximity feature until Canon introduced a proximity aligner in the 1970s.

Henderson found that Kasper's failure in this generation came because it did not understand that a proximity aligner required a different relationship between the components than did a contact aligner. She points to two illustrations of this. In response to complaints about its product, Kasper diagnosed the problem as a "processor error." This diagnosis was common for contact aligners, and so Kasper inferred it was at work for the new aligner. The problem was that a component in the new aligner, while adequate for contact alignment, was not of sufficiently high quality for proximity alignment. Kasper devoted few resources to that component, a mistake that cost it the market share that Canon managed to capture. Another illustration was Kasper's response to Canon's introduction of proximity alignment. Kasper evaluated this using the same criteria as it had used to evaluate its own aligners, but, as it turned out, Canon had made significant advances that Kasper's engineers did not see or dismissed as unimportant.

The same sequence hit market leaders for subsequent generational changes as well. Perkin-Elmer, the leader in scanning projection aligners, lost its position when stepper technology took off in the 1980s. Its engineers had evaluated both technologies, forecasting the improvement in individual components but not in their interaction. And the firm that disrupted Perkin-Elmer, GCA, later repeated Perkin-Elmer's failed evaluation when Nikon introduced a second-generation stepper machine.

Echoing Kasper, GCA first pronounced the Nikon stepper a copy of its own design. Even after GCA fully recognized the threat posed by the second-generation stepper, it was handicapped by its historical experience in its attempts to develop a competitive machine. GCA's engineers were organized by component, and cross-department communication channels were structured around the architecture of the first-generation system. While GCA engineers were able to push the limits of the component technology, they had great difficulty understanding the advances in component integration that had given Nikon's aligner its superior performance.[4]

This experience supports the theory of supply-side disruption: when faced with architectural innovations, market leaders that optimized their processes based on the existing generation were unable to adapt and compete in the new generation. This provided an opportunity mostly for entrants. I say "mostly" because even in photolithographic alignment, there was an exception to the rule: Canon.

Canon's Integrated Approach

We have seen that firms in the photolithographic alignment industry often failed to make the transition between different architectures. Consequently, market leadership was fleeting. By contrast, the Japanese multinational Canon defied this trend and successfully introduced products in more than one generation of the technology.[5] How did Canon achieve this?

One thing it did not do that others in the industry did was set up a skunk works. As Henderson observed, "[n]ew ventures may move faster and take more risks: but if the designers continue to rely on tacit architectural knowledge, the group is likely to fail."[6] This happened in photolithographic alignment equipment and "several skunkworks engineering projects failed miserably" by relying on historical architectural knowledge. There was, in fact, a case in which integration was so undervalued that "the product could not even be assembled successfully—its parts did not fit together!"

By contrast, Canon's product development organization played by the best-practices handbook: "It used heavyweight project managers and tightly knit teams. It cultivated close links to customers. Its engineers were committed to the success of the semiconductor equipment business as a whole."[7] While one possibility is that Canon simply had better product development managers than its rivals, it is worth bearing in mind that Canon never led the market technically or otherwise for any given generation of technology. Instead, Canon invested in different generations of technology at the same time and ensured that key personnel had experience in each. This investment had a long time horizon, which also meant that Canon often lagged others in bringing new products to market.[8]

Canon was an assiduous follower; for example, it introduced a proximity printer in 1976 and a scanner in 1978. Though both products lagged the competition by two years, the delay came with the benefit of forcing Canon's engineers to understand their competitors' equipment. They needed to find an improvement to give them a competitive advantage. Thus, for both the proximity printer and scanning projection, Canon used an alignment system it developed internally that was different from the systems developed by its competitors. In effect, by simultaneously developing products over two generations, Canon forced itself to understand their architecture more deeply and to innovate on architectural knowledge. When it came time to introduce a stepper, Canon came into the market six years after its competitors. However, because of its superior knowledge of that technology, it was still able to secure a solid market footing.

In the weeds of product development, introducing architectural innovations regularly was achieved by top management having a very hands-on approach with the development team—again something diametrically opposed to an autonomous approach. So while competitors focused their energies on single generations, Canon's senior management pushed experimentation across multiple generations. This gave Canon a wider product range but also helped precisely because the industry was subject to continual waves of disruption. Had there only been a single architectural innovation, this strategy would less likely have shown up as profitable in the long term.

Canon also was heavy-handed in its allocation of personnel to product development tasks. It continually rotated experts among different disciplines—moving the optical designers so they could learn as much as possible about the mechanical and electronic aspects of products. This also allowed for tighter integration between design and manufacturing. But a complement to this eschewing of the division of scientific labor was ensuring that those with general skills would have authority. So while the task of achieving integration among component teams was a challenging one and likely frustrating for some on a day-to-day basis, the long-run effect was to prepare Canon to embrace new innovations more readily.

The Canon experience introduces a philosophy for insurance against supply-side disruption: instead of exploiting a given architecture through specialized autonomous units innovating on components, firms will invest in an integrated structure that embeds architectural knowledge in the minds of as many people as possible, thereby allowing that knowledge to evolve and change. This means that the firm will have a greater chance of sustainability across technological generations but is unlikely to be a leader in any one. It is also not apparent that this is necessarily a more profitable strategy, just a distinct one. It is important to note that academic research regarding how to insure against supply-side disruption has not advanced much beyond this point. The case of Canon points to the value of engaging in cross-generational research in a more or less simultaneous manner but also emphasizes the way in which "taking your time" can assist in sustainability.

In summary, while demand-side disruption involves an established firm missing a certain kind of technological opportunity, supply-side disruption arises when an established firm becomes incapable of taking advantage of a technological opportunity. Specifically, when a new competing innovation involves a distinct set of architectural knowledge, established firms that have focused on being "best in breed" in terms of component innovation may find it difficult to integrate and build on the new architecture.

Nonetheless, the insurance premium for supply-side disruption involves reduced performance. In order for an organization to employ and "remember" architectural knowledge, those responsible for the components need to be reminded of how their choices interact with the choices of others.[9] Thus, the firm has to be more tightly integrated so that important tacit knowledge can be absorbed and retained in the organization. This effort of integration can divert resources and attention away from traditional component innovation activities and thus may reduce firm performance at any given point in time.

Integrative Capabilities

While the Canon case shows the benefits of integration for ensuring that architectural innovations can be absorbed into an organization's product development team, the benefits in terms of insuring against disruption can go further. In particular, in some situations firms will want to absorb resources—particularly talent, skills, and technology—from outside their organizations in order to anticipate or deal with disruption. By also pursuing integration within their organizations, they can develop experience and capabilities that allow them to integrate these external resources.[10]

To see this, I want to return to the case of Mergenthaler that was examined in chapter 4. Recall that the typesetting industry underwent waves of radical innovation that completely devalued the existing assets of incumbent firms bar one: their proprietary font libraries. Fonts bought the initial hot-metal incumbents breathing room. When analog typesetting technology emerged, they had time to work out their strategies, and it was the choices they made at that point that drove their futures. Mergenthaler, Intertype, and Monotype all introduced machines based on the new technology. Critically, Intertype launched its machine first while Mergenthaler, after feedback from its customers, delayed introducing a new machine for a decade. In other words, it chose to trust its good management instincts rather than rush to market.

It had good reason to be cautious. As Mary Tripsas, who studied this industry, carefully documents, almost nothing of value from hot-metal typesetting (other than the fonts) transferred over to phototypesetting. For instance, while hot-metal was exclusively based on mechanical engineering, she estimates that such skills were only useful for about 10 percent of what was required in later generations (which relied on electronics knowledge). How was this additional knowledge acquired? Mergenthaler, after failing to build a new machine on its own, acquired talent externally and used an integrated team to build the next-generation machine. By contrast, Intertype moved quickly by dealing with external partners (e.g., Kodak) to graft the new technologies onto its existing machines. This turned out to be insufficient. So while Mergenthaler faced a tough transition, transition it did—remaining the market leader. Intertype and Monotype fell by the wayside.

What Mergenthaler was able to do by focusing on integrating new knowledge and skills into its existing teams was to develop what Tripsas called "external integrative capability." This allowed the firm to monitor and then take on new technologies as they emerged around the world in a variety of industries (especially information technology) and acquire talent to ensure that these new technologies could be developed internally in conjunction with existing capabilities. As the pace of major technological change accelerated, Mergenthaler went from strength to strength and was able to ensure that its extensive font library continued to be leveraged to its fullest. Its competitors never had that focus and so proved not to be resilient through the new technological changes that awaited.

This highlights an additional way in which integration can forestall disruption alongside the simultaneous development of multiple technological generations. Following the move from hot metal to phototypesetting, Mergenthaler developed external capabilities in integration. Its goal was to ensure that it was able to absorb and then integrate any new technologies that might come its way. This involved having not only outward-looking engineering and development teams, but also a willingness to acquire new skills and technologies and immediately look for ways of developing them alongside their existing product development operations. Interestingly, this process slowed Mergenthaler down. It was never the first to market with a new typesetting technology and did not achieve the dominant heights it had reached in the hot-metal days, but it was able to move from one technological generation to another and maintain market leadership.

In this regard, Mergenthaler's key asset, its font library, gave it an incentive to leverage that asset itself. While, in principle, one can imagine such an intellectual property asset existing independently of a typesetting business, Mergenthaler found advantages in being able to supply typesetting machines to key publishers who had already specialized in its fonts. The advantage of this, as opposed to divided supply of fonts and machines, is that Mergenthaler could more easily transact and price a single product. In the modern parlance, *it owned the customer experience*. This was likely advantageous both to itself and to its customers. Indeed, it was only when the machines themselves became less necessary with full digital typesetting that Mergenthaler (or more specifically the later owners of its font assets) moved to a business model that involved licensing its font library rather than embedding it in equipment.

Integration as Identity

Both Mergenthaler and Canon demonstrate that firms can continue to retain a focus on their customers' needs and that, so long as they take a broad approach to assimilating technologies—even if this sacrifices speed to market—they can ride disruptive waves. In their cases, the final products were very similar in function to the preceding generation's, while it was the underlying technology in promoting that function that changed. For film manufacturers transitioning to digital technology, however, the products had fundamentally changed. Fujifilm—and its rivals Polaroid and Kodak—faced challenges that drove to the heart not only of their organizations but also of how the organizations were formed around their business models. This required a deep and evolving change in organizational structure in order to deal with the disruption that came in the form of digital photography.

As already discussed, both Polaroid and Kodak failed to make the transition from film to digital photography. In their cases, while each anticipated digital trends, internal conflicts made it difficult to move and then organize for an alternative business model that did not have high margins from film as a revenue source. What is instructive is that Fujifilm was able to move beyond such conflicts. While never the leader in its market, it successfully transitioned from the film to the digital world and remains a strong performer today.[11] Like Canon, what Fujifilm did and others did not is pursue an integrated approach. What is interesting here is how it did so.

Mary Tripsas, whose work uncovered Mergenthaler's key to success, later took a very close look at Fujifilm's identity. She argued that when a firm establishes an identity that highlights and can accommodate the changing technologies and markets in an industry, it can orient itself to manage resource conflicts that inevitably arise without having to sacrifice the firm's strengths.

In the 1980s, Fujifilm's leadership saw the changes that were coming to film and set the company on a path to redefine itself as an "imaging and information" company. Like its competition, Fujifilm also realized the potential of digital technology early on. It began research in digital photography in 1975 and produced prototype products in the early 1980s. While its main sales were in film, photographic paper, and photographic chemicals, Fujifilm also had businesses in x-ray film and processors, microfilm, graphic arts films, magnetic tape, and carbonless copying paper.[12] This breadth turned out to be critically important. In 1978, Fujifilm explicitly changed its identity from being photography-focused to being "an integrated audio-visual information recording company."[13] This was actually part of a longer strategic process that had moved its business definition from photography to "image."

Tripsas argues that this orientation mattered for Fujifilm's choices. For instance, it was able to launch hardware for electronic radiography at a higher price point rather than stick to the "razor and blade" business model that had characterized device pricing when film could be sold. In other words, Fujifilm's identity assisted management in considering and implementing new business models suited for the digital world.

Moreover, research organizations within Fujifilm and its competitors took very different paths. For example, Fujifilm's digital imaging units were integrated with the main R&D division whereas Polaroid's were distinct units. This gave Fujifilm's digital imaging units legitimacy and minimized conflicts. Over the years, Fujifilm began to realize that the core of the company included specialty chemistry in addition to imaging and that this new core might lead to new opportunities. Thus, as imaging required less chemistry, Fuji's chemical expertise found new support, though this was still closely connected to imaging. For example, the firm explored applications of Fujifilm's chemistry to generate outstanding digital images on displays (key components for televisions and computer screens), pharmaceuticals, and cosmetics.

By becoming an "information and imaging" company, Fujifilm was able to transition to the digital realm in ways its competitors failed to do. This allowed its digital endeavors to be integrated, and thus opened the company to new opportunities.

PowerPoint versus Excel

Because we normally think of insurance as being worth it, it is tempting to make the same evaluation regarding insuring against disruption. But as we have shown, there is likely a premium to be paid in terms of reduced performance and a lower rate of profitability. Firms might choose (or be forced by competitive pressures) to structure their organizations to take more or less insurance against disruption. Thus, it is instructive to consider those choices and when a firm might choose one path over another.

As already argued, different ways of approaching organizational structure can lead to very different outcomes. Before considering this in the context of insuring against disruption, it is useful to take a step back and consider precisely how the structure of communication channels—both quantitative and qualitative—can impact organizational performance.

Janet Vertesi is a Princeton sociologist who has made a career of conducting analyses of teams in NASA by being embedded within them for significant periods of time. A recent study of hers looks at the "social life of robots," or more precisely of the people who control them.[14] Vertesi has studied various NASA interplanetary teams that are comprised of a robot sent out into space and a team of scientists on earth telling the robot what data to collect. All the while, teams are subject to difficult choices to ensure that the robot does not die.

In the course of her study, Vertesi examined two different teams with robots exploring two different planets. I'm going to call them Team PowerPoint and Team Excel.[15] On Team Excel, the robot has a number of instruments but separate teams manage and have property rights over those instruments. The structure is hierarchical, and the various assignments the instruments are given are mapped out in Excel. By contrast on Team PowerPoint, no one team owns an instrument. Instead, all decisions regarding, say, where to position the robot are made collectively in a meeting. The meetings are centered around PowerPoint presentations that focus on qualitative tradeoffs from making one decision rather than another. Then decisions are taken using a consensus approach—literally checking if everyone is "happy."

What is fascinating about this is that the types of data collected by each team are very different. On Team Excel, where each instrument is controlled and specialized to its task, the data from them is very complete and comprehensive on that specific thing—say, light readings, infrared, etc. On Team PowerPoint, there are big data gaps for each instrument but there appear to be more comprehensive, deep analyses of a particular phenomenon, in which all of the instruments can be oriented toward the measurement of a common thing. This is a classic tradeoff between specialized knowledge and deep knowledge. And it is a tradeoff that each of these missions needs to make. What is extraordinary is that they bake the tradeoff into their organizational structure and also their decision-making tools.

There are other interesting elements in this. For instance, different disciplines associated with different teams are more likely to collaborate on scientific publications in Team PowerPoint than in Team Excel. Also, there is a different philosophy of commons ownership, with the entire robot being owned in common in Team PowerPoint whereas individual instruments are owned in Team Excel. But conflicts in Team Excel can arise and are resolved by various trades predicated on a strange nonsharing norm in their own data economy. In other words, they default to property rights and the market. By contrast, Team PowerPoint shares everything—even with the public.

From this, it sounds like Team PowerPoint is more functional, and it was easy to get that impression. But the important take-away is that the data being collected by each team was very different. We tend to think of there not being much choice regarding precisely what scientific information will be collected during space exploration missions. In this case, the choice of organizational structure led to very different outcomes. Our knowledge of one planet will be very different from our knowledge of another, due to choices not about what data to collect but how to collect it.

The Real Dilemma

The distinction between Team PowerPoint and Team Excel is not unlike the distinction between firms whose product development teams are highly integrated and those whose teams are not. Team Excel was operationally efficient but rigid in dealing with change. Team PowerPoint was flexible but left opportunities on the table as it chose to explore some paths based on consensus and not others that might have deepened specific scientific knowledge. These are metaphors for the choice firms face in whether to be tightly integrated (operating like Team PowerPoint) or focused on performance (operating like Team Excel).

In making a choice about insuring against disruption, as with any insurance, you have to consider the risk you are trying to handle. Many of the firms that have been considered in this book—Blockbuster, RIM, Kodak, Britannica, the New York Times—were challenged by a single disruptive event. For other industries—typesetting, photolithographic alignment equipment, hard disk drives—there were multiple waves of disruptive or architectural innovations. In those industries, firms would have come to see the risks of disruption as much higher, even though a single disruptive event could pose an existential threat in any industry.

What this suggests is that, other things being equal, integration is a price worth paying when an industry is subject to waves of potentially or actually disruptive events. In this situation, if you did not pursue integration and went for market leadership and performance, that period of leadership would likely be relatively short-lived. By contrast, in industries that appear to be more stable in their technologies, the value of insurance is reduced and more firms might choose to do without.

Even so, I do not wish to claim that insuring against disruption and adopting tighter integration in your innovation teams will leave your firm on smooth waters. Doing so should put it in a position to manage disruption and respond to it, but even this process could leave your business in a markedly different form as the tide changes, as the more recent history of Mergenthaler shows.

In 1997, Mergenthaler Linotype became Linotype Library, a spun-out company that housed its extensive font library that had only grown over the years. In 2005, it became part of Boston-based Monotype Imaging.[16] By that time, print media were on the way out, and the earlier decision to focus just on the fonts was prescient. Put simply, there was no long-term role for the machinery of print any more.

So, given this, was Mergenthaler's integration strategy worth it? More than a century of market leadership suggests that it was. But more critically, during that period it controlled the look of the published word, and that look persists on the web and in digital media today. Indeed, it is arguable that this is why Linotype's fonts are still so valuable and that this new era is just one more successful transition to add to its record. In 2015, Monotype Imaging/Linotype acquired Swyft Media, a leading supplier of emojis (little pictures that carry meaning) to companies such as Disney, Sony, and Dreamworks.[17] This suggests that its journey will continue for some time yet.

8

Reexamining Disruption

One of the reasons I chose to write this book was that the theory of disruption has evolved since Christensen's 1997 book. However, his work and the evidence it presents are still the sole source from which many managers learn about the theory, become convinced that it is real, and consider their options. It is a touch point for conversations and common ground for many.

At the same time, two decades is a long time in management. As I have already outlined, even before and concurrent with Christensen, others had additional, possibly competing, perspectives on disruption. Moreover, many actions have been taken in the name of disruption that are not at all related to the ideas put forth in *The Innovator's Dilemma*. For this reason, I want to take a moment in this chapter to revisit the industry that spurred the disruption discussion and debate: the hard disk drive industry.

Christensen first developed his demand-side theory of disruption while studying the hard disk drive industry. What he found, circa 1992, was a turbulent industry with changes in leadership occurring alongside a very dynamic set of technological changes. After observing the ebb and flow over the course of a few years, he asked industry insiders what was going on, and found them perplexed because they thought they had been in control. Using the lens of demand-side disruption, Christensen was able to link disruptive innovations to market leaders stumbling and, in some cases, failing.

However, many other academics have studied this industry, using the same data, and have come to conclusions inconsistent with Christensen's. In some cases, they found incumbent strength rather than failure; in others, they concluded that managerial experience was an asset rather than a liability. Yet another set of studies saw more going on than simple entry and exit, finding a raft of acquisitions, consolidation, and a production pipeline that spanned the world. Given these findings, it is hardly surprising that, looking back at hard disk drives, some believed that the simple relationship Christensen initially drew between disruptive innovation and incumbent failure did not seem strong.[1]

This chapter, then, will reexamine the hard disk drive industry and what it can tell us about disruption. We will find that it can tell us a lot, even if the message is not one that Christensen emphasized. Indeed, it is an industry that touches on each of the issues dealt with in previous chapters, which is why academics have paid it so much attention over the last 25 years. For this reason I have set aside examination of it until this point: to use it as a capstone case to summarize what we have learned about disruption.

A Remark on Testing Theories

This chapter is about using evidence to assess theories. Thus, it is necessary to pause and consider when a theory is useful. To a scientist—social or otherwise—a theory can only be useful if it has testable implications. That is, it must be possible to conceptualize experiments in which one outcome would be consistent with the theory and another would prove it false.

Theories regarding disruption involve some disruptive event—for instance, the appearance of a new technological opportunity with certain properties followed by the failure of a previous successful firm(s)—coupled to some causal mechanism that explains this failure. To test a theory, we have to look not only to situations where firms fail but also, perhaps more importantly, to situations where they don't fail, and see whether the disruptive event took place in these instances. It is not enough, when we hear about a successful firm's failure, to try to identify after the fact some event as the disruptive trigger. This approach is often fraught with recall bias, and by itself is not solid evidence for the theory of disruption at all. For a theory to have power, it needs to produce specific predictions before any test is carried out, and the test itself must be designed so that the theory can potentially be rejected.

What this means, of course, is that even when we observe outcomes consistent with a theory, we can never be sure that our particular theory is at the heart of those outcomes. The only thing we can be sure of is that when we observe outcomes inconsistent with a given theory, this particular theory has been proved false.

To test any theory, we need to find overall patterns and identify a common or dominant mechanism for disruption. This requires us to look beyond individual cases of successful-firm failure; we need observational data on a defined environment over a sufficiently long time period in which we can expect some firms to become successful and then also to fail. The problem is that, for different industries, disruptive events may not come that often, making it hard to look for patterns.[2]

So what environment can we look at for evidence? The demand-side theory of disruption implies that successful firms that pay close attention to their existing customers are the most vulnerable to failure. To test this theory, we need to find a setting where we can examine technological or other innovations in an industry and determine whether they satisfied the two criteria of (1) initial underperformance and (2) rapid improvement. If we found that successful firms were *at least as likely* to fail when faced with either type of innovation (those satisfying and those not satisfying these criteria), this would count against the hypothesis that successful firms were *more likely* to fail when faced with disruptive innovations than with sustaining ones.

In his PhD research, Christensen looked to the hard disk drive industry as an appropriate test bed for understanding the failure of successful firms. Indeed, he later referred to disk drive firms as the "fruit flies" of innovation and management studies, as, he believed, no firm managed to persist as a market leader for more than a few years. But as turbulent as the industry has been, it has also been relentlessly innovative. When Christensen published his study of the industry in 1994, the price per MB of hard disk space had been falling at an exponential rate for two decades. (Whatever else was going on in the industry, it appeared that the outcome was great for consumers.) Because the industry had seen many innovations in the span of a few decades (including a few that could be uncontroversially classified as disruptive innovations), it seems an appropriate place to look for evidence backing the demand-side theory of disruption.

Even in an industry that has had many disruptive events, it can be difficult to stand back and let the data speak for itself. Indeed, throughout this book, I have used individual cases as a way of motivating and then adjusting the broader theory of disruption. While the theories of both demand- and supply-side disruption may have started from a simple relationship between a disruptive event (i.e., an innovation type) and the failure of successful firms, the cases have yielded what Christensen has described elsewhere as "anomalies" that did not reflect that simple relationship.[3] For this reason, I and many others have augmented and adjusted the simple relationship to a theory that is more complex so as to account for these anomalies and, indeed, absorb them or de-anomalize them. This activity is common for many academics when teaching cases and also for many managers in trying to understand the world, but it does not reflect the usual scientific method. That method requires you to state a hypothesis, test it, and then, if it is rejected by the evidence, to stop believing it. In practice, a rejection leads to further refinement, which can be incremental or drastic, leading to a new theory and then further tests. Stated this way, perhaps the main difference between hypothesis rejection and adjusting theories based on an anomaly is the size of the sample that leads to a change in position. Even through the exercise of writing this book, I have not been pure in applying the scientific method and have used cases to motivate, speculate, and provoke thought; and I will, in part, do so again in this chapter.

Do Entrants Introduce Disruptive Innovations First?

In the demand-side theory of disruption, it is new entrants that initially bring disruptive innovations to market, while established firms are responsible for introducing sustaining innovations. In this section, we will see whether that theory is borne out in the evidence from the hard disk drive industry.

Let's begin with the classification questions. To test the demand-side theory of disruption we need to know (i) which innovations were disruptive and which were sustaining, and (ii) which firms were entrants and which firms were established incumbents at the time innovations appeared. Christensen undertook the painstaking task of classifying technological innovation, noting the tradeoff between disk size and performance and identifying several step changes in disk size (that is, discrete changes in the size of drives). In each size change, the move to a smaller drive led to lower storage capacity and therefore initially to reduced performance. However, the trajectory for performance improvement was faster on the smaller drives than the larger ones. Thus, while it was always the case that 5.25-inch drives had a lower capacity than their 8-inch counterparts, the gap was closing year on year. Consumers did not have to sacrifice as much in capacity to obtain a smaller and possibly more energy-efficient drive.

Christensen argues, convincingly, that capacity was a key performance metric for mainstream customers, while the small physical size appealed to what were then niche customer segments. For instance, in 1980, while

8-inch drives were demanded by minicomputer manufacturers, 5.25-inch drives were more attractive to the growing niche of personal computer makers who were looking for units with a smaller footprint. For this reason, it is reasonable to classify these step changes in physical size as disruptive innovations. By contrast, there were hundreds of other improvements to the components of disk drives introduced by different companies that were instead sustaining innovations.

On the firm side, Christensen examined the outcomes for 77 entrants into the US hard disk drive industry between 1971 and 1989 (excluding those integrated with computer manufacturers). He defined "success" as a firm achieving in excess of $50 million in sales in at least one year of its operations (in 1987 dollars). Firms that failed to do so were accordingly defined as "failures," whether they exited or were still operating as of 1989. Of course, successful firms could also withdraw from the market, and, from the perspective of looking at disruption, it is those firms that are of primary interest.

Table 8.1 lists those size innovations, the market leaders at the time they were introduced, and the firms that introduced them. Of these innovations, it was nonestablished firms that first brought the 8-inch, 5.25-inch, 3.5-inch, 1.8-inch, and 1.3-inch drives to market. I say "nonestablished" because often the firms involved, while relatively new to the industry, were not new entrants: most of them had, in fact, launched products in the previous generation. However, the remaining four of the nine disruptive innovations listed here were introduced early on by established firms in the industry.

The very first instance of a "smaller" drive—14 inches—was introduced by IBM, an established firm. The 2.5-inch, 1-inch, and 0.85-inch drives were likewise introduced by established firms. From this we can interpret that *disruptive innovations tend not to be introduced by established firms (compared with sustaining innovations) but are not exclusively introduced by entrants*. In fact, in some cases established firms were able to lead innovation for new products serving niche customer classes (although arguably those may have been cases where there was a relatively small difference between the new generation and the current generation).[4] Thus, the broad conclusion is that Christensen was correct that disruptive innovations favored initial entrant leadership.

Did Disruptive Innovations Lead to Incumbent Failure?

Of course, the demand-side theory of disruption does not simply say that nonestablished firms are more likely to introduce disruptive innovations

Table 8.1
Disruptive Innovations in Hard Disk Drives since 1973

New Size	Date	Leading Incumbents	Innovating Firms
14-inch	1973	Control Data, ISS, Burroughs	IBM
8-inch	1978	Control Data, Diablo, Memorex	IBM, International Memories, Shugart Associates, Priam
5.25-inch	1980	Control Data, Century, Memorex	Seagate, Tandon, International Memories, Rodime
3.5-inch	1983	Control Data, Seagate, Priam	Rodime, Microcomputer Memories, MiniScribe
2.5-inch	1989	Seagate, Conner, MiniScribe	Prairie Tek, JVC, Conner
1.8-inch	1991	Seagate, Conner, Maxtor	Integral Peripherals
1.3-inch	1992	Conner, Seagate, Quantum	Hewlett-Packard
1-inch	1998	Seagate, Quantum, Western Digital	IBM
0.85-inch	2004	Seagate, Western Digital, Maxtor	Toshiba

Note: Data compiled from Christensen, "The Rigid Disk Drive Industry, 1956–90"; Rick Farrance, "Timelines: 50 Years of Hard Drives," *PC World,* September 13, 2006, accessed July 5, 2015, http://www.pcworld.com/article/127105/article.html; McKendrick, Doner, and Haggard, *From Silicon Valley to Singapore,* and *Disk Trend* reports. The rules for the construction of this table were as follows: (i) the market leaders were the three firms with the largest market shares in the noncaptive markets; and (ii) the innovating firms were those that shipped a drive of that size within a year of the first shipment.

than established firms: it also says that established firms will lose their market position permanently as a result of that force, displaced by smaller and newer counterparts. These entrants, after securing a foothold with a new customer segment, will improve their performance and start to compete for the established firms' existing customers.

The hard disk drive industry up until 1992 was very turbulent. In fact, of all the firms that had a role in this industry in the early 1970s, only one (IBM) still had a role 20 years later. The market leader during the initial period—indeed, all the way until 1986—was Control Data Corporation. Its dominant Winchester design was integrated into most mainframes and minicomputers, but ultimately Control Data Corporation lost its market share and lead to Seagate. At the time, Seagate was a new entrant that came in with the 5.25-inch drive and was one of the first to target hard drives for the personal computer market. The PC market turned out to be the largest downstream market for hard disk drives (with recent sales of mobile devices shifting demand to solid-state and flash-based drives). As the demand-side theory would predict, no firm that was a significant producer in the 8-inch segment managed to make the transition and become a significant independent competitor in the 5.25-inch market. Control Data Corporation was eventually bought by Seagate in 1989, although it was still the second largest manufacturer of hard disks at the time of acquisition.[5]

Apart from Seagate there were two other successful entrants during the period examined: Conner Peripherals, which entered with the 3.5-inch drive, and Western Digital toward the end of the period. At first glance, Seagate, Conner Peripherals, and Western Digital seem to fit the criteria for disruptive new entrants, but for a full picture we need to understand the founding stories of these three firms.

Seagate (then Shugart Technology) was founded in 1979 by Finis Conner, Syed Iftikar, Doug Mahon, Tom Mitchell, and its namesake and perhaps most famous cofounder, Al Shugart.[6] Shugart was one of the great entrepreneurs in computing. He started his career with an 18-year stint at IBM, where he helped develop some of the first disk systems before leaving in 1969 to join Memorex. He took several hundred IBM engineers with him, surely enough for us to call Memorex a spin-out of IBM. Memorex played an important role in the 14-inch systems, but Shugart himself left in 1972 to form Shugart Associates. This was one of the entrants responsible for introducing the 8-inch drive. Shugart was actually forced out by the board of his company in 1974 and took a five-year break from the industry. He returned with a new company, Seagate, after cofounder Finis Conner (a colleague from Memorex) convinced him that there was an untapped opportunity in the disk drive industry. In 1980, just a year after its founding, Seagate introduced the very first 5.25-inch disks to the industry. Shugart was to stay at Seagate for the rest of his disk drive career. Seagate cofounder Finis Conner, however, only stayed until 1985.

After founder disagreements, Conner resigned from his role as CEO and later that year founded Conner Peripherals.[7] This company merged with two incumbents in the industry and became a leading supplier of 3.5-inch drives. In its time, Conner Peripherals was the fastest-growing manufacturing start-up in US history. In 1996, Conner and Shugart again became colleagues as Seagate merged with Conner Peripherals. Today, Seagate remains the largest of the three remaining hard disk drive manufacturers in the market (along with Western Digital and Toshiba).

As for Western Digital, its story was relatively long and slow. It was founded in the 1970s as an integrated circuit manufacturer and made several abortive attempts to enter into data storage in the 1980s. In 1988, however, it acquired the hard drive facilities of Tandon (a personal computer manufacturer) and started making external drives for those computers.[8] Over time, Western Digital grew, notably acquiring IBM's hard drive division in 2002 and then in 2012 acquiring Hitachi's 2.5-inch, 3.5-inch, and other drive divisions.[9] Unlike the other entrants into this industry, Western Digital did not enter by way of a new disruptive innovation, but instead with products and capabilities achieved through targeted acquisitions.

Suffice it to say, the complex backgrounds of these seemingly "disruptive new entrants" do not reinforce the very simple demand-side theory of disruption that Christensen has argued for. Christensen interpreted the industry's history as providing four cases where the step changes in disk drive size caused incumbents to misstep by listening too closely to their existing customers, eventually losing market share to new entrants. Though he was correct that new entrants were responsible for most of the disruptive innovations, in most cases they did not end up changing the overall market leadership in the industry. There are several factors at play that suggest why the simple demand-side story does not hold up.

First, it is fair to say that, when it comes to analyzing sustainability of competitive advantage, time can reveal some truths not apparent when an analysis was conducted. Bower and Christensen, in 1995, wrote that Seagate had "been reduced to a shadow of its former self in the personal-computer market." Seagate certainly had some issues in the early 1990s, lagging in entry into the 3.5-inch market. But it was still the leading manufacturer of disk drives, and, as history now shows, it continued to be a sustained market leader over the next two decades. Moreover, despite entering later, Seagate made strategic moves to catch up and became the leader in the 3.5-inch market through superior supply chain management and efficiency that allowed it to bring high-quality but lower-cost units to market.[10] An observer of Seagate in 1998 would come to a very different conclusion about the firm's future than Bower and Christensen did in 1995.

Second, the demand for disk drives was changing very rapidly over the period Christensen studied—more so perhaps than it did subsequently, at least for computers. Minicomputers challenged mainframes and were in turn challenged by personal computers and then portable computers. In each case, the industry moved from platform to platform—not just the hardware but the software ecosystem as well.[11] In the traditional demand-side story of losing by listening to your existing customers, the challenge comes because of rapid improvement by otherwise inferior products. In disk drives, however, the tradeoffs that customers had to make between physical size and virtual size were less salient; if you had a computer that could house a larger drive, this was still the dominant characteristic. Thus, in the 1990s, drives of all sizes had places in the market—and more importantly, each had its own distribution and marketing channel. It is that feature that made it difficult for established firms to control the market, as it was not just technology that was evolving but the entire architecture of the ecosystem.

Christensen's narrative concluded that different-sized drives appealed to different markets, and that entrants were able to successfully capture new markets with smaller drives. However, as McKendrick, Doner, and Haggard demonstrated, existing firms like Control Data, IBM, Century Data, and Digital Equipment had great success selling 14-inch drives to minicomputer manufacturers.[12] In fact, when the 8-inch market finally launched, it was comprised right from the start mostly of firms that had made 14-inch drives, including IBM, which was no nimble entrant.[13]

The one case where we see Christensen's original theory supported by the historical record is the move to the 5.25-inch drive size, in which entrant Seagate targeted the PC market and grew to dominate incumbents Quantum, Micropolis, and Control Data. This demonstrates to me that disruption as a phenomenon was present in the industry even if it did not play out in terms of failure as consistently as a reader of Christensen in 1997 might have appreciated.

Finally, the standard demand-side theory of disruption does not include the influence of talent and people. April Franco and Darren Filson have demonstrated that the new entrants that were responsible for introducing disruptive innovations were invariably formed by employees of a then-incumbent firm.[14] Al Shugart moved from IBM to Memorex, then formed Shugart Associates and then Seagate. Along the way, he brought substantial engineering talent with him, including Finis Conner who went on to cofound Seagate with him and then Conner Peripherals. The 1996 merger of Conner Peripherals and Seagate formed the largest hard disk drive manufacturer. Shugart, Conner, and a few of their senior employees rode the wave from 14-inch drives all the way down to 1.8-inch drives. These examples represent the norm rather than an anomaly.

Such leadership experience prevented their companies from failing to respond to innovations; instead they were often early entrants into new product fields. This suggests that managers had a great role in promoting the sustained competitive advantages of established firms. Of course, this also suggests that management actions may help explain why otherwise potentially disruptive events did not lead to disruption.

In the end, the picture we have of the hard disk drive industry is closer to a picture of many emergent markets: customers make a new demand—in this case, for independently manufactured hard disk drives—there is a considerable amount of entry into the industry, followed by a considerable exit, or "shakeout," from that industry. Eventually, the industry matures and settles down with a relatively stable set of market leaders. This has been the story of the second two decades of the disk drive industry, with the caveat that the movement of top personnel played a key role in the entry and promotion of some of the more significant innovations in the industry. Thus the case of the US disk drive industry, long upheld as the standard of demand-side disruption, actually reveals a much more complicated view of disruption than previously understood.

The Replacement Effect

In light of the discussion of the replacement effect in chapter 5, let us canvas the hard disk industry for evidence that, rather than listening too much to their customers and choosing not to adopt crucial innovations, incumbents were thinking about the replacement effect and had an insufficient incentive to move quickly. It may also just be that the incumbents were sluggish and faced higher costs in adopting these innovations, perhaps because there were architectural elements in the innovations that favored entrants. Again, an examination of the hard disk drive industry can tell us something about these competing explanations.

We have already noted that the industry's move from 5.25-inch to 3.5-inch drives was rather slow, the first such drive being introduced three years before Conner established a solid market presence (followed in turn by Seagate which later dominated that segment). Mitsuru Igami[15] recently examined this particular instance using the very same *Disk*

Trend dataset used by Clayton Christensen for his PhD work.[16] Igami considered a model that took into account many competing theories, including the replacement effect and also both theories of disruption, to suggest that incumbents have higher costs than entrants do in adopting step jumps in innovation (like the move from 5.25- to 3.5-inch drives). Specifically, Igami wanted to measure just how much of a delay (if any) between entrants' and incumbents' new product launch times is explained by replacement incentives as opposed to differences in costs. As it turns out, for this specific instance in hard disk drive history, none of the delay (or to be precise a negative amount of the delay) was explained by an incumbent cost disadvantage. In fact, incumbents had lower costs, something that is not surprising given our earlier finding that this particular change was not associated with a very large change in customers downstream (i.e., both 5.25- and 3.5-inch drives served the personal computer market). Instead, 66 percent of the gap between entrant and incumbent launch dates was explained by the replacement effect. This reinforces my earlier contention that replacement should be a natural part of any theory of disruption.

Doubling Up and Acquisition

The analysis in this chapter shows that while it was entrants that often introduced disruptive innovations in hard disk drives, this did not necessarily result in incumbent failure. In chapter 5, we offered two explanations for this potential pattern: that established firms doubled up and invested more heavily than entrants once an innovation was revealed to be disruptive; or that they acquired those entrants. We begin here by considering doubling up and what the data shows in that regard.

Harvard Business School's Josh Lerner examined the disk drive industry in research conducted in the early 1990s using the same *Disk Trend* dataset used by Christensen and Igami. In contrast to other researchers, his focus was on competition within a particular disk drive size category rather than between sizes. Lerner was attracted by the intense advances in the industry in the 1970s and 1980s as well as the fact that many of the underlying innovations were not subject to strong patent protection. This set the stage for a set of technology races for market leadership. Lerner wanted to see who would win in such races: those that were first to market with a new disk class or those that followed the technology leaders.

After an exhaustive examination, Lerner came to a clear conclusion: in hard disk drives, it was the followers rather than the leaders that invested most in new disk drive classes and consequently ended up as the market leaders.[17] Specifically, for any given drive diameter, Lerner ranked all of the products in the market according to the density of the drive (that is, how much you could squeeze onto a drive of that physical size). The leaders were those in the top 25 percent of products in that class, and the followers were the rest. While the leaders did innovate, they were consistently outinnovated by the followers. As we know from Christensen's classification (and also Igami's analysis), new entrants were the most likely to introduce a new size class. Lerner's analysis suggests that the established firms that followed were indeed doubling up as their strategic response to potential disruption. Moreover, their subsequent success suggests that this response, while it may have been costly to achieve, was effective in forestalling potential disruption.

The evidence supports a similar conclusion with regard to acquisition as a successful strategy in managing disruption. Seagate dominated the hard disk drive industry in the late 1990s with its version of the 3.5-inch drive. However, its path to that position was not a smooth one. As Christensen extensively documents, other firms had launched 3.5-inch drives first while Seagate was focused on the previous 5.25-inch model. One of the firms to beat Seagate to the 3.5-inch market was Conner Peripherals.[18] Conner's own 3.5-inch drive was by then among the market leaders. However, in 1993, perhaps due to competitive pressure, Conner made a loss of $445.3 million and was falling behind in generating a leading product.[19] Or maybe, as Christensen argued, it was that Seagate was feeling the competitive heat from Conner. Regardless, in September 1995, Seagate agreed to purchase Conner for $1.1 billion. That move caused share prices of all drive manufacturers to rise: something economists see as an indication that the move may be about reducing rather than increasing competition.[20]

This incident suggests another way in which an established firm can manage disruption as it occurs: by buying up the new entrants. While one might argue that this strategy on the part of Seagate involved significant doubling up prior to a deal being struck with Conner, the notion of waiting and then purchasing the competition is consistent with demand-side disruption at the very least. By waiting, an established firm can see whether its own customer base is threatened by the new entrant. By purchasing that entrant as things become clearer, the established firm can then manage the disruption. Indeed, for Seagate, this appears to have been a pattern. It purchased Control Data in 1989, Maxtor in 2006,[21] Samsung's drive division in 2011,[22] and LaCie in 2012.[23] Maxtor itself had been an acquirer of competitors, including MiniScribe in 1990[24] and Quantum in 2000.[25] All told, Seagate was responsible for the exits (directly or indirectly) of nine of its rivals by acquisition.

Is Disruption Related to Experience?

What about proactive managerial actions in the context of disruption in the hard disk drive industry? Christensen's key thesis may have been that success made firms vulnerable to failure. One way of thinking about this is to consider whether experience—as measured at the level of the people in a firm—is related to the failure of incumbent firms.

Fortunately, using the same *Disk Trend* report data as Christensen and others, Andrew King and Chris Tucci conducted a broad statistical analysis of the drivers of exits of hard disk drive manufacturers between 1976 and 1995,[26] a period that covers all of the industry's disruptive technologies analyzed by Christensen. King and Tucci were interested in the role of managers in ensuring the long-run sustainability of firms. Recall that the demand-side theory of disruption suggests that managers may be the problem; the best and most experienced managers have knowledge and communication channels to their mainstream customers and may rationally ignore opportunities to develop disruptive innovations that do not appeal to those customers. In particular, King and Tucci looked at *experience* in the previous generation as a predictor of firm success in the next generation (i.e., in the next hard disk drive size). What they found is that, contrary to what would be expected under demand-side disruption, experience in the immediate past generation (as measured by the firm's sales in that generation, cumulative sales, or its experience with transitions) was positively correlated with success in the next generation. This was also the case if the firm was entering new niche markets of the industry. They concluded that "management experience" should be viewed as a complementary asset that can help sustain firms through otherwise difficult technological transitions. Moreover, Franco and Filson found this conclusion to hold up when looking at managers who switched to new entrants: individual management experience in earlier phases of the industry proved an indicator of future success.[27]

Since the analysis indicates that management experience may be a benefit rather than a hindrance in the hard disk drive industry, it is possible that this very experience assists firms in making difficult spin-out decisions to transition from one disruptive technology to the next. In a follow-up paper, King and Tucci took this thesis head-on and coded their data to include whether hard disk drive makers had spinoffs or not.[28] They found that whether a firm had a spin-out or not did not impact its probability of surviving disruptive innovation on average. Moreover, the spin-outs themselves had a higher probability of exiting than entrants did. Of course, it should be noted that King and Tucci were looking at all firms rather than just the most successful ones, and it may be that the spin-out option is of value only to the market leaders.

So what type of experience can assist in the survival of incumbent firms in the face of disruption? The thesis proposed in this book (notably in chapter 7) is that incumbents can insure against disruption if they develop integrative experience and capabilities. While these options are costly, there is a sense in which they are a built-in means of insurance. Moreover, firms that build experience and capabilities either in doubling up or in acquiring other firms will reduce the chances that demand-side disruption will fell them later. The notion that a firm can develop capabilities for doubling up and acquisition when challenged by disruptive technologies is best exemplified by the hard disk drive manufacturer Seagate. Seagate's strategy, as expressed by its cofounder, focused "not [on] who is there first, but who can support the quantities needed with a quality product."[29] As McKendrick, Doner, and Haggard painstakingly documented, success in hard disk drives was driven by the ability to develop a supply chain capable of handling the explosive growth in the computer market throughout the 1990s and 2000s. This required scaling manufacturing facilities beyond North America to Southeast Asia. Indeed, Seagate built up that supply chain capability, eventually becoming the largest private employer in Singapore, Thailand, and Malaysia and China's largest exporter during the 1990s.[30] This ability to be a low-cost, large-scale supplier allowed Seagate to double up when it started making smaller drives. Moreover, the consolidation of that production chain allowed it to be a consistent acquirer and integrator of other firms and their own Southeast Asian facilities, including Conner and Maxtor. In effect, from this perspective Seagate developed proactive capabilities in being a manager of demand-side disruption, and arguably this was responsible for its continuing success to this day.[31] While they do not constitute insurance per se, these continual investments demonstrate that it is possible to manage your way into sustainability in the face of disruptive innovations.

Was Supply-Side Disruption at Play?

Thus far, we have found that there was, in the terms of the demand-side theory of disruption, only one truly disruptive event in disk drives over the critical period from the mid-1970s to the mid-1990s. It occurred when Seagate introduced the 5.25-inch hard drive to target personal computers rather than minicomputers. The fact that the key customer changed in that transition is suggestive of demand-side forces at work. However, it is useful to wonder—especially given the importance of integrative capabilities thereafter—whether there were supply-side disruptive forces at work in the hard disk drive industry as well.

The answer turns out to be affirmative and to come from an unlikely source. In 1998, Christensen along with Fernando Suárez and Jim Utterback published a paper reexamining the hard disk drive industry from a dominant design perspective.[32] Recall that we looked at this perspective in chapter 3 when discussing why the iPhone architecture had such an impact on the mobile handset industry. Once the iPhone appeared, smart phones coalesced around that design; those that didn't eventually left the industry.

Christensen, Suárez, and Utterback argued that the same pattern could be seen in hard disk drives, although in that case the dominant design took a decade to emerge. The dominant design was introduced in 1984 by Maxtor which incorporated two architectural innovations and two component innovations. Half a decade later all manufacturers had adopted this design. Of key interest are the two architectural innovations. The first was the Winchester architecture developed by IBM in 1973 that encased all the hard disk components in a dust-free housing, increasing speed and accuracy. The second was the under-spindle pancake motor. Seagate introduced this in 1980 as the only way to spin the disks themselves inside its small 5.25-inch pack. Both of these were architectural in nature as they significantly changed the way the components of the drive interacted with one another.

What is significant here is that the only truly disruptive event, which led to the failure of all incumbent firms operating before that point, was associated with an innovation that was architectural in nature. To be sure, it was a disruptive technology as well; but this goes to prove that disruption theory has multiple flavors, and consequently that we need to take them all into account in any analysis of turbulence in an industry.

Disruption, Evidence, and Management

The purpose of this chapter was to revisit the seminal story of disruption and evaluate whether the facts on the ground match up with many long-held beliefs about the hard disk drive industry. Though popular thought would have you believe that disruption occurred many times in this industry in the 1980s and 1990s, it is difficult (as shown here) to come up with evidence of systemic disruption. For disk drives, there was only one clear instance of disruption, in the move from 8-inch to 5.25-inch disk drives associated with the move from larger computers to personal computers. But for other industry changes, entrants sometimes moved more quickly to new segments than incumbents. Here it appears that the firms that most listened to their customers did worse than stumble because of it.[33]

The message this leads to is one of *hope* rather than *fear*. If disruption is a real phenomenon that cannot be managed, then successful firms have a "use by" date and their leadership should be fearful. But the evidence here tells a different story and suggests an evolution in how we should think about disruptive forces. The fact that firms were not necessarily disrupted in a systematic and ongoing way does not mean that disruption itself is not a legitimate concern. Instead, firms may find ways either to manage that disruption reactively or to take steps proactively to mitigate the worst consequences of potential disruption. The reason failure and exit did not systematically appear in the disk drive industry is not that demand-side disruptive forces were absent, but rather that successful firms and market leaders found ways to maintain their leadership. Thus, the anomalies to the simple, initial theory of disruption can be somewhat accounted for by considering both demand- and supply-side sources of disruption as well as the range of actions that managers facing disruption have at their disposal.

9

Future of Disruption

In the closing minutes of the original *Star Wars* movie,[1] a subordinate officer approaches the Death Star's leader, Grand Moff Tarkin. "We've analyzed their attack, sir, and there is a danger. Should I have your ship standing by?" Tarkin responded "Evacuate? In our moment of triumph? I think you overestimate their chances!" Suffice it to say, David slew Goliath a few minutes later.

Business is rarely one decision away from destruction, but complacency can be a trap. More critically, the small can topple the large, the weak can take out the strong, and success seems always to come with an end date. Those whose work led up to what we now call the theory of disruption, from Schumpeter to Foster to Christensen and Henderson, each gave support to the idea that those at the top are not as secure as many, especially they, believe. Small wonder, therefore, that Intel's Andy Grove came to live by the mantra "only the paranoid survive."

The problem today is that we have moved from Tarkin-like complacency to Grove-like paranoia while the truth is somewhere in between. This has led to a trend of crying wolf at purported disruption everywhere. Many have chosen to torture the theory until it confesses that, yes, whatever firm *seems* like it is currently on top is only a few short moments away from doom. In my opinion, that has led to distraction and mistakes, clouding the value of the underlying ideas.

The Apple in Your Eye

The best way to illustrate the attempt to fit facts to a theory is to consider how many have analyzed the future prospects of Apple. At the time of writing this book, Apple is the world's most valuable company; naturally, it is a target for numerous prophecies of its demise.[2] In this regard, I will examine Christensen's attempts to employ his theory of disruption in predicting that demise. To be fair, he was doing this long before Apple was anywhere near its modern heights, and it is possible that he holds different opinions today. His public statements about Apple, however, mirror the conversations I have had in day-to-day interactions with many business leaders, and so they are an important place to start.

At the time Christensen wrote the *Innovator's Dilemma*, Apple was a shadow of its former self and had just failed to ignite the personal digital assistant market with its Newton product. It was reasonable to think that Apple's star had forever dimmed, and Christensen suggested that the company was another victim of disruption. As we now know, Apple had a stunning resurgence in the late 1990s with the return of Steve Jobs, which management scholars have been trying to unpack ever since. By 2006, Apple had launched a successful new product category with its iPod that proceeded to transform the music industry. Christensen did not see this success lasting. He believed that Apple's proprietary system—including its own player, format, digital encryption, and music store—would not last as the product became more modular. Other competitors with good music players would compete with Apple on price, and eventually Apple would lose its competitive advantage: "Apple may think the proprietary iPod is their competitive advantage, but it's temporary. In the future, what will matter will be the software inside that lets users find exactly the kind of music they want to listen to, when and where they want to, with minimal effort."[3]

His solution was for Apple to open up and bring iTunes to all music players, something Steve Jobs never did. Many have been hard on Christensen about this.[4] After all, no MP3 player managed to challenge the iPod, and Apple was not disrupted by a new entrant. But it is interesting to note that Christensen was right in a sense. On the issue of whether you could bring non-Apple-sold music onto an Apple device, Apple answered in 2007. With the launch of the iPhone, the music-playing iPod became just an app; the iPhone could play music from many digital sources. In particular, thanks to improvements in mobile broadband and cloud services, the music industry moved to a streaming/subscription model through apps on Apple (and other) devices.

Because the iPhone was not tied to music and Apple wanted to sell more iPhones, Apple let competition for music reign even to the detriment of its own music business unit. It could easily have kept prohibiting music from competitors on its iPhone, allowing Apple to extend market power through bundling. Why did Apple choose against that? Because it did not see itself as in the music business and instead was doubling up on making its mobile devices better. In a sense, Apple managed its way out of what might have been potential disruption by turning away from the replacement effect earlier than many would have expected. Even today it continues to do so, this time via acquisition, with its purchase of Beats Music for almost $3 billion.[5] With regard to the iPod, Christensen may have well been right about the risks Apple faced. What he did not touch on was that disruption could be managed.

Turning to the iPhone, in 2007 Christensen was clearer in predicting its failure.[6] As we discussed in chapter 3, Christensen saw the iPhone as a sustaining innovation, although there were lower-end features (poor call quality, no keyboard) that might make an observer think of it as disruptive. Christensen himself admitted later that his initial classification of the iPhone was wrong. This illustrates that the difficulty of classifying a technology before the fact is one of the main reasons why it is so hard to determine whether a disruptive event is taking place. I wonder whether an additional error was in not recognizing the iPhone as a new product architecture. As explained in chapter 3, this is why no incumbent mobile handset manufacturer managed to succeed in replicating Apple's new mobile dominant design while many entrants did. New architectural innovations are perhaps even harder to identify at the time than new disruptive ones, precisely because what makes the architecture work can be hidden from established players that have organized around previous architectures.

In 2012, Horace Dediu, a long-standing and well-respected analyst of Apple, asked Christensen to explain why Apple does not seem to fit the theory of disruption.[7] Christensen attributed it to Apple's lucky streak of finding new products it could pursue a proprietary model in:

The transition from proprietary architecture to open modular architecture just happens over and over again. It happened in the personal computer. Although it didn't kill Apple's computer business, it relegated Apple to the status of a minor player. The iPod is a proprietary integrated product, although that is becoming quite modular. You can download your music from Amazon as easily as you can from iTunes. You also see modularity organized around the Android operating system that is growing much faster than the iPhone. So I worry that modularity will do its work on Apple.[8]

In my opinion, this focus on proprietary versus open architectures seems to be out of place, and emphasizing luck does not seem to be right.

To understand my perspective here, let's consider the advantages of having a proprietary or highly integrated approach, as Apple did during its most successful periods. The key element is control; by having control over many elements of its products and the surrounding ecosystem, Apple can make large changes without significant adverse effects. It allows management to coordinate multiple innovative projects simultaneously across divisions. For example, Apple initially wanted to make a tablet before realizing that the iPhone was a more immediate opportunity. After launching the iPhone, Apple turned its attention back to the tablet market. This was a market many had tried to break into with a dominant design and had failed; as compared to a computer, it requires architectural rather than a modular innovation. But because of its integrated hardware and software design team and its shared developer community, Apple was able to launch the iPad with an interface and experience that users were accustomed to on the iPhone. It is hard to remember that Apple was late to the tablet market, but that is the hallmark of companies (like Canon) that use integrated approaches to ensure deep architectural knowledge of their products.[9]

Similarly, if we return to the Encyclopaedia Britannica example that opened this book, control from an integrated, proprietary approach can play an important role in a firm's ability to rapidly innovate. Encyclopaedia Britannica relied on third parties for sales, employing highpowered incentives (e.g., large commissions). That meant fundamental changes to the product were extremely costly to implement. By contrast, Apple controlled the sales channels more carefully. Apple Store employees, for example, were not paid bonuses, so they did not worry if there were changes to the product line-up. This made it much easier for Apple to engage in drastic product changes.

Thus, on the one hand, it is right to say that Apple used the proprietary model, and that can be useful when launching new product categories. On the other hand, the App Store and its resulting ecosystem represented a clear move toward modularity. All app developments are modular innovations relative to Apple's mobile technologies. With over a million apps, it can hardly be called closed, especially in comparison to the operator-controlled mobile app space that existed prior to the iPhone. To emphasize this point another way, open approaches do tend to be more flexible in exploiting modular innovation, as Christensen states. Android has allowed many experiments including specially designed operating systems by Facebook, Amazon, and Xiaomi, which has allowed Android to be quicker to market with keyboard innovations, wearable devices, and phones of different sizes.[10] The difference is that Apple has built a system by which it can explore new architectures freely and patiently relative to others, while keeping some parts of its platform open. Hence, Apple will launch new products later to market than others.

All of this does not mean that Apple is invulnerable. To see this, let's turn to another tech titan, Microsoft. Where Apple has succeeded by seeming to invest in architectural knowledge and by not being concerned with the replacement effect, Microsoft has in many ways done the opposite. It has invested in capabilities that allow it to more effectively manage its way through disruptive events. We saw in chapter 5 that, when faced with the threat of the web browser, Microsoft doubled up and won the resulting browser wars. It had done this repeatedly with graphical user interfaces (i.e., Windows), media players, search, an entire office software suite, video games, even encyclopedias (just to name a few). In each case, entrants established the market before Microsoft realized the opportunity and aggressively competed for those markets. The end result is that while it has had its ups and down, in 2014 it emerged again as the second most valuable company in the world, behind Apple.

What does this mean for Apple? Apple's strategy for avoiding disruption has been two-pronged. One might argue that it avoids demand-side disruption by never listening to its customers and instead building products it believes are top-quality.[11] Famously, Apple has never used focus groups or other traditional customer-oriented product development tools. That is not to say that it does not adopt innovations its customers want; it just does not do it with urgency. This was true, for instance, of multitasking on its mobile devices, keyboard options, and more recently a larger screen size for phones and a smaller one for tablets.

On the supply side, as we have seen, Apple's highly integrated approach to product innovation on multiple fronts has given it arguably deep architectural knowledge about its own product areas. In those areas where it has succeeded, no one has appeared to catch up to it at the high end of the market. But at the same time, the theory tells us that there is a potential vulnerability. What will happen if someone else develops a new product architecture? Will Apple be able to assimilate it?

There is no answer to this question, and arguments can be made either way. On the negative side, Apple has faced issues that were unresolved as of the writing of this book. For instance, it moved relatively late in developing its own maps product,[12] which led to uncharacteristic disappointment from its customers. Apple has also struggled with cloud services for the better part of a decade. Even after Steve Jobs claimed that the cloud was the hub of the Apple product system on the launch of iCloud, it is safe to say that these services are not fully adopted as intended.[13] That said, many large tech companies are struggling with this, although Microsoft has actually managed to grow cloud services with a massive investment in Azure. Unlike Microsoft, Apple simply does not have the same capabilities in doubling up.

A complete theory of disruption needs to recognize both the demand- and supply-side processes as well as the various insurance and management options available to established firms. This provides a more accurate picture of Apple in terms of successes and also potential threats to its future. Put simply, Apple has insured itself by pursuing integration in a deeper manner than most other tech firms, which at the same time has allowed it to look past the replacement effect in launching new products. As there is no perfect insurance option, Apple is still vulnerable to disruptive events that require reactive management. It is these that we should pay attention to in the future.

Reconstituting Disruption

This book has attempted to deconstruct and then reconstruct our understanding of the phenomenon of disruption. The hope was to provide a complete picture of the phenomenon that went beyond that of any single theory.

The task began with a clear but restricted definition of disruption. Disruption is a phenomenon whereby firms are found to falter precisely because they are pursuing the choices and strategies that made them successful. Disruption of this kind can be so severe that firms fail because of it. Encyclopaedia Britannica, Blockbuster, Nokia, and Kodak are all examples of this. What is interesting is that, in each of these cases, what came to be the disruptive event was known to the firms involved and in some cases extensively acted upon, but to no avail. That said, when we turned to look at evidence of disruption, there was no reliable association between defined disruptive events and disruption to the point of failure. There were other things going on.

One of those things was other *complementary assets* that firms possessed that allowed them to ride out disruptive events. These assets—such as the library of fonts held by typesetters—meant that while disruptive events could cause firms competitive harm, they also provided them leverage to come back and continue to lead their markets. Often they would be a locus of consolidation in the industry, with technological leadership perhaps changing but market leadership remaining somewhat stable.

Another factor was that, at least under the demand-side theory of disruption, established firms have options to *manage* their way through disruption after the fact. To be sure, the replacement effect gives established firms reasons to slow down the impact of disruption, or at least not accelerate it by their own actions. However, once the disruptive event is out of their control, their incentives switch to either doubling up on the new technological trajectory or, alternatively, acquiring entrant competitors. When academics reexamined the hard disk drive industry and also the speech recognition industry for the application of these strategies, they found that the strategies were pursued especially when associated with disruptive events. Thus, the reason why disruptive events could not be systematically linked to disruption may be that firms learned to manage their way through them.

A final factor that might explain why potentially disruptive events do not always lead to disruption is the preemptive action that firms sometimes take to insure against the consequences of disruption. For instance, they may invest in independent divisions to insure against demand-side disruption or in integrated research agendas to insure against supply-side disruption. Each of these involves ongoing costs and constraints that might harm a firm's competitiveness over time. However, it is also possible for firms to strengthen their ability to manage disruption as they gain experience in doing so. Over time, they may acquire capabilities for doubling up or acquiring entrants. These capabilities may shape whether or how disruptive events impact those firms.

All this leads to a more complete picture of disruption. Rather than focusing on whether disruption exists or is important, this picture allows business leaders to think about their firm's orientation for dealing with disruption. Will they use proactive or reactive management to deal with demand- or supply-side disruption? Can they accept lower short-term competitive advantage in return for greater sustainability? And can they develop the experience necessary to deploy strategies to successfully manage through disruptive events?

Ultimately, the message is that successful firms and their investors can calm down. This does not mean they can relax; there is always much to be done. But academic research and market experience demonstrate that the fear of inevitable and imminent disruption is unfounded.

Notes

Preface

1. Clayton Christensen, *The Innovator's Dilemma* (Boston: Harvard Business School Press, 1997).

2. This is only true in the main, and especially in the term's translation into popular parlance. As I will discuss, some academics—including Erwin Daneels, David McKendrick, Richard Doner, Stephan Haggard, Andy King, and Chris Tucci—did, in fact, challenge Christensen in academic journals.

3. Toni Mack, "Danger: Stealth Attack," *Forbes*, January 25, 1999, accessed July 5, 2015, http://www.forbes.com/forbes/1999/0125/6302088a.html.

4. Christensen is often at pains to explain that he did not persuade Grove of this but instead conveyed his theory to him and that Grove did the rest.

5. Marc Andreessen (@pmarca), "15/To be AGAINST disruption is to be AGAINST consumer choice, AGAINST more people bring served, and AGAINST shrinking inequality," December 2, 2014, 9:10 a.m., tweet; Marc Andreessen (@pmarca), "16/If we want to make the world a better and more equal place--the more Christensen-style disruption, and the faster, the better!," December 2, 2014, 9:11 a.m., tweet.

6. Interestingly, for a word that is now used with abandon, *disruption* is itself relatively new to the world of management scholarship. For instance, it did not appear in Christensen's 1992 Harvard doctoral thesis (Clayton M. Christensen, "The Innovator's Challenge: Understanding the Influence of Market Environment on the Processes of Technology Development in the Rigid Disk Drive Industry," PhD/DBA diss., Harvard University Graduate School of Business Administration, 1992) and was only introduced in his 1995 *Harvard Business Review* article (with Joseph Bower) in the context of "disruptive technology." (Joseph L. Bower and Clayton M. Christensen, "Disruptive Technologies: Catching the Wave," *Harvard Business Review* 73, no. 1 [January 1995]: 43–53.) Prior to that article, the term was on the fringe of management vocabulary, and was more likely to have been used to describe a weapon in *Star Trek*, by teachers describing rambunctious schoolchildren, or by travelers lamenting delays at airports.

Chapter 1

1. Shane Greenstein and Michelle Devereux, "The Crisis at Encyclopaedia Britannica," Kellogg School of Management, Northwestern University, Case No. 251 (2009).

2. Josh Goldstein, "Surprising Lessons from a 20th Century Encyclopedia Salesman for Client Protection Today: A Holiday Parable," *Centre for Financial Inclusion blog,* December 14, 2010, accessed July 5, 2015, http://cfi-blog.org/2010/12/14/surprising-lessons-from-a-20th-century-encyclopedia -salesman-for-client-protection-today-a-holiday-parable.

3. This was written on the announcement in 2012 that *Britannica* would no longer have a print edition. Michael Milton, "Elegy for an Encyclopedia Britannica Salesman," *Michael Milton blog,* March 16, 2012, accessed July 5, 2015, http://michaelmilton.org/2012/03/16/elegy-for-an-encyclopedia-britannica -salesman.

4. Greenstein and Devereux, "The Crisis at Encyclopaedia Britannica."

5. "Encyclopædia Britannica," Wikipedia, accessed July 5, 2015, http://en .wikipedia.org/wiki/Encyclop%C3%A6dia_Britannica.

6. "U.S. Households with a Computer in the United States (Fee-Based)," Statista, accessed July 5, 2015, http://www.statista.com/statistics/184685/ percentage-of-households-with-computer-in-the-united-states-since-1984.

7. Robert Calem, "Get Smart—at Any Age—with Digital Encyclopedias," *BusinessWeek,* October 14, 1998, accessed July 5, 2015, http://www .businessweek.com/cbguide/1998/mav81014.htm.

8. Greenstein and Devereux, "The Crisis at Encyclopaedia Britannica."

9. This analysis has benefited considerably from conversations with Shane Greenstein and Scott Stern.

10. "History," Matson Corporation, accessed July 5, 2015, http://www.matson .com/corporate/about_us/history.html.

11. For an account of these changes see Joshua Gans, "Inside the Black Box: A Look at the Container," *Prometheus* 13, no. 2 (December 1995): 169–183; Marc Levinson, *The Box: How the Shipping Container Made the World Smaller and the World Economy Bigger* (Princeton: Princeton University Press, 2006).

12. US regulations prohibited cross ownership of companies in different transport modes.

Chapter 2

1. Matt Phillips and Roberto A. Ferdman, "A Brief, Illustrated History of Blockbuster Which Is Closing the Last of Its US Stores," *Quartz,* November 6, 2013, accessed July 5, 2015, http://qz.com/144372/a-brief-illustrated-history -of-blockbuster-which-is-closing-the-last-of-its-us-stores.

2. Willy Shih, Stephen P. Kaufman, and David Spinola, "Netflix," Harvard Business School, Case No. 607-138 (2007, 2009).

3. Netflix did, in fact, have a patent on its model, resulting in litigation with Blockbuster that was eventually settled for a relatively small payment by Blockbuster.

4. My editor pointed out to me that usually the key mentor (like Alfred or Uncle Ben) doesn't wear a cape.

5. I could say the same thing but I don't know how to ride a horse.

6. Joseph A. Schumpeter, *The Theory of Economic Development: An Inquiry into Profits, Capital, Credit, Interest and the Business Cycle*, trans. Redvers Opie (1911; New Brunswick, NJ: Transaction Publishers, 2008).

7. Joseph A. Schumpeter, *Capitalism, Socialism and Democracy* (New York: Harper, 1942), 83; emphasis in original.

8. I write "easily," but there were some hiccups on the way as Netflix tried, unsuccessfully, to separate its DVD rental and video streaming businesses.

9. Giovanni Dosi, "Technological Paradigms and Technological Trajectories," *Research Policy* 11 (1982): 147–162.

10. Richard N. Foster, *Innovation: The Attacker's Advantage* (New York: Summit Books, 1986).

11. James M. Utterback and William J. Abernathy, "A Dynamic Model of Product and Process Innovation," *Omega* 3, no. 6 (1975): 639–656.

12. Joseph L. Bower and Clayton M. Christensen, "Disruptive Technologies: Catching the Wave," *Harvard Business Review* 73, no. 1 (January 1995): 43–53.

13. Clayton M. Christensen and Michael Raynor, *The Innovator's Solution* (Boston: Harvard Business School Press, 2003).

14. Specifically, cable television companies rolled out their own video-on-demand services and had access to recent releases often a year or more before Netflix did. The same was true for services like Apple's iTunes.

15. Richard Oppel Jr. and Andrew R. Sorkin, "Enron's Collapse: The Overview; Enron Corp. Files Largest U.S. Claim for Bankruptcy," *New York Times*, December 3, 2001, accessed July 5, 2015, http://www.nytimes.com/2001/12/03/business/enron-s-collapse-the-overview-enron-corp-files-largest-us-claim-for-bankruptcy.html.

16. Andrew Wahl, "Nortel: Collapse of a Giant," *Canadian Business*, January 14, 2009, accessed July 5, 2015, http://www.canadianbusiness.com/technology-news/nortel-collapse-of-a-giant.

17. For that reason, great firms are usually the ones you have on your own list, and that list is certainly shaped by your personal baggage. Christensen's 1997 book started by thinking about greatness. Sears Roebuck (at its 1960s peak accounting for 2 percent of US retail sales) was introduced on page 1 and its failure documented by page 2. He then follows with IBM, Digital Equipment Corporation, Xerox, and Apple. Apple is an interesting case. At the

time of writing this book, Apple is the world's most valuable company, but for Christensen, writing almost two decades earlier, Apple had been great but no longer was. Clayton M. Christensen, *The Innovator's Dilemma: When New Technologies Cause Great Firms to Fail* (Boston: Harvard Business School Press, 1997), 1–2.

18. Although in the case of Enron it is hard to tell. It may be that these accounting practices were at the heart of the firm's success, but I think we can agree that it wasn't transparently so.

19. Actually, this more nuanced argument was developed not by Christensen but by Ron Adner; we will discuss it in more detail in chapter 3. Ron Adner, "When Are Technologies Disruptive? A Demand-Based View of the Emergence of Competition," *Strategic Management Journal* 23 (2002): 667–688.

20. See Matt Marx, Joshua Gans, and David Hsu, "Dynamic Commercialization Strategies for Disruptive Technologies: Evidence from the Speech Recognition Industry," *Management Science* 60, no. 12 (2014): 3103–3123, for the development of this argument.

21. Clayton Christensen, "Clayton Christensen's 'How Will You Measure Your Life?'," *Harvard Business School*, May 9, 2012, accessed July 5, 2015, http://hbswk.hbs.edu/item/7007.html.

22. "Blockbuster to Rent through New On-Demand Device," *USA Today*, November 25, 2008, accessed July 5, 2015, http://abcnews.go.com/Technology/story?id=6366022.

23. Austin Carr, "Blockbuster Bankruptcy: A Decade of Decline," *Fast Company*, September 22, 2010, accessed July 5, 2015, http://www.fastcompany.com/1690654/blockbuster-bankruptcy-decade-decline.

24. R. Thomas Umstead, "Blockbuster-Enron Deal Fades to Black," *Multichannel News*, March 19, 2001, 32.

25. Michael Liedtke and Mae Anderson, "Blockbuster Tries to Rewrite Script in Bankruptcy," *Boston Globe*, September 23, 2010, accessed July 5, 2015, http://www.boston.com/business/articles/2010/09/23/blockbuster_tries_to_rewrite_script_in_bankruptcy.

Chapter 3

1. Matthew Honan, "Apple Unveils iPhone," *PC World*, January 9, 2007, accessed July 5, 2015, http://www.macworld.com/article/1054769/iphone.html.

2. The term "effectively failed" may seem inflammatory here. All of these firms are still around, but it is safe to say that their handset businesses are a shadow of what they used to be. That said, some of these businesses do have alternative assets that are still of value—for instance, Nokia is still a leading manufacturer of cellular phone network technology.

3. Jena McGregor, "Clayton Christensen's Innovation Brain," *Bloomberg Business*, June 15, 2007, accessed July 5, 2015, http://www.businessweek.com/

stories/2007-06-15/clayton-christensens-innovation-brainbusinessweek-business
-news-stock-market-and-financial-advice. Let me put my own cards on the
table here. I saw the 2007 keynote from Steve Jobs introducing the iPhone and
thought it was the most amazing thing I had ever seen. I remarked on that at
the time (Joshua Gans, "Apple Does It Again," *Core Economics blog*, January
10, 2007, accessed July 5, 2015, http://economics.com.au/?p=577) and saw
the trajectory going right to the iPod (Joshua Gans, "Apple: Beyond the
Computer," *Core Economics blog*, January 11, 2007, accessed July 5, 2015,
http://economics.com.au/?p=581). Then again, *Business Week* wasn't asking for
my opinion.

4. Stuart Dredge, "Nokia Responds to Apple iPhone—'It Is a Surprise That
the iPhone Is Not 3G,'" *Tech Digest*, January 2007, accessed July 5, 2015,
http://www.techdigest.tv/2007/01/nokia_responds.html.

5. Jay Yarrow, "All the Dumb Things RIM's CEOs Said While Apple and
Android Ate Their Lunch," *Business Insider*, September 16, 2011, accessed July
5, 2015, http://www.businessinsider.com/rim-ceo-quotes-2011-9?op=1. There
were also reports that RIM did not believe the iPhone was possible and that
Apple were not showing a real product. ("RIM Thought iPhone Was
Impossible in 2007," *MaCNN*, December 27, 2010, accessed July 5, 2015,
http://www.electronista.com/articles/10/12/27/rim.thought.apple.was.lying.on
.iphone.in.2007). It turns out they were partly right! But a working iPhone
did launch on schedule. Fred Vogelstein, "And Then Steve Said, 'Let There
Be an iPhone,'" *New York Times*, October 4, 2013, accessed July 5, 2015,
http://www.nytimes.com/2013/10/06/magazine/and-then-steve-said-let-there-be
-an-iphone.html?pagewanted=all&_r=3&.

6. Steve Ballmer (CEO, Microsoft): "There's no chance that the iPhone is
going to get any significant market share. No chance. It's a $500 subsidized
item. They may make a lot of money. But if you actually take a look at the 1.3
billion phones that get sold, I'd prefer to have our software in 60% or 70% or
80% of them, than I would to have 2% or 3%, which is what Apple might
get." Cade Metz, "Tech Time Warp of the Week: Watch Steve Ballmer Laugh at
the Original iPhone," September 5, 2014, accessed July 5, 2015, http://www
.wired.com/2014/09/tech-time-warp-of-the-week-watch-steve-ballmer-laugh
-at-the-original-iphone.

7. When asked about his earlier mistake, Christensen admitted his
misjudgment but then argued instead that the iPhone was "disruptive to
laptops." Jon Gruber wrote in 2012 that Christensen was correct to consider
that the iPhone disrupted portable computers as it was, in fact, a computer.
While that might be the case, laptop makers do not appear to have failed as a
result of these changes, even if we generously consider the iPad as a larger
iPhone. Larissa MacFarquhar, "When Giants Fail," *New Yorker*, May 4, 2012,
accessed July 5, 2015, http://www.newyorker.com/magazine/2012/05/14/
when-giants-fail. John Gruber, "The iPhone and Disruption: Five Years In,"
Daring Fireball blog, July 2, 2012, accessed July 5, 2015, http://daringfireball
.net/2012/07/iphone_disruption_five_years_in.

8. Clayton M. Christensen, *The Innovator's Dilemma: When New Technologies Cause Great Firms to Fail* (Boston: Harvard Business School Press, 1997), xv; emphasis in original.

9. In doing this, he drew from the work of Jeffrey Pfeffer and Gerald Salancik, *The External Control of Organizations: A Resource Dependence Perspective* (New York: Harper and Row, 1978).

10. Jesse Hicks, "Research, No Motion: How the BlackBerry CEOs Lost an Empire," February 21, 2012, accessed July 5, 2015, http://www.theverge.com/2012/2/21/2789676/rim-blackberry-mike-lazaridis-jim-balsillie-lost-empire.

11. Ibid.

12. RIM did not stand still, however. Apple had signed a four-year exclusive deal with AT&T in the US, a deal that Verizon had passed on. Verizon was desperate to come up with a consumer-oriented device to prevent a flow of customers to its rival. RIM obliged and quickly developed the BlackBerry Storm. It looked like an iPhone with a large touch screen but had a distinctive BlackBerry flavor. In particular, it was uncompromising in terms of how it continued to use RIM's own server-oriented connectivity and economized on battery life and bandwidth. The touch screen had a tactile effect of clicking when pressed to give people the sense they were typing with a physical keyboard. Verizon embraced the Storm as did customers when it was launched in 2008 (just over a year after the iPhone). But the rush to market took its toll. The device was flawed; the sturdy manufacturing of the BlackBerry was lost and most had to be returned with large costs to both Verizon and BlackBerry. This set RIM back years in developing its proper response to the iPhone with its new operating system, BlackBerry 10. See Jacquie McNish and Sean Silcoff, *Losing the Signal: The Untold Story behind the Extraordinary Rise and Spectacular Fall of BlackBerry* (New York: HarperCollins, 2015).

13. Brian Chen, "June 29, 2007: iPhone, You Phone, We All Wanna iPhone," *Wired*, June 29, 2009, accessed July 5, 2015, http://www.wired.com/2009/06/dayintech_0629.

14. Christensen later admitted that Adner's insights were, in fact, valid and changed his own thinking regarding the mechanisms of his theory.

15. Ron Adner, "When Are Technologies Disruptive? A Demand-Based View of the Emergence of Competition," *Strategic Management Journal* 23 (2002): 667–688.

16. Fred Vogelstein, "The Day Google Had to 'Start Over' on Android," *Atlantic*, December 18, 2013, accessed July 5, 2015, http://www.theatlantic.com/technology/archive/2013/12/the-day-google-had-to-start-over-on-android/282479.

17. Carriers like Verizon helped out here by actively promoting the initial Android phones—notably Motorola's Droid (which included a physical keyboard)—as they hoped to stem the tide to AT&T during its period of iPhone exclusivity.

18. Moreover, Android itself couldn't provide RIM with the security it needed to serve its longstanding customers. Thus, there was no simple solution like just adopting Android that was available.

19. Thom Patterson, "DC-3: The Unbelievable Airliner That Just Won't Quit," *CNN*, June 4, 2014, accessed July 5, 2015, http://www.cnn.com/2014/06/04/travel/aviation-douglas-dc-3.

20. It is useful to observe that when it comes to text entry, Apple did, in fact, adopt RIM's pioneering approach of a limited QWERTY keyboard designed for a two-thumb approach to text input. Hence, that key design feature for BlackBerry has survived up until the present.

21. Armen Alchian, "Uncertainty, Evolution and Economic Theory," *Journal of Political Economy* 58 (1950): 211–221; Milton Friedman, *Essays in Positive Economics* (Chicago: University of Chicago Press, 1953).

22. Christensen was himself quite aware of that tradition and sought to distinguish his approach from it. That is why the demand-side theory that I have already outlined focuses outward toward the customer and how this impacts on managerial choices rather than on the internal mechanisms of adjustment. That said, Christensen did, at times, evoke the supply-side tradition, which is one of the reasons why, until now, it has been hard to separate them.

23. Kenneth J. Arrow, *The Limits of Organization* (New York: Norton, 1974).

24. Variants of this idea were put forward by Paul R. Lawrence and Jay Lorsch, "Differentiation and Integration in Complex Organizations," *Administrative Science Quarterly* 12 (1967): 1–30; Jay Galbraith, *Designing Complex Organizations* (Boston: Addison-Wesley Longman, 1973).

25. Rebecca Henderson and Kim B. Clark, "Architectural Innovation: The Reconfiguration of Existing Product Technologies and the Failure of Established Firms," *Administrative Science Quarterly* 35, no. 1 (1990):13.

26. Nicolaj Siggelkow used a similar framework to analyze the rise, fall, and resurgence of Liz Claiborne. Nicolaj Siggelkow, "Change in the Presence of Fit: The Rise, the Fall, and the Renaissance of Liz Claiborne," *Academy of Management Journal* 44, no. 4 (August 2001): 838–857.

27. Henderson and Clark, "Architectural Innovation," 18.

28. Ian Austen, "Bowing to Critics and Market Forces, RIM's Co-Chiefs Step Aside," *New York Times*, January 22, 2012, accessed July 5, 2015, http://www.nytimes.com/2012/01/23/technology/rims-jim-balsillie-and-mike-lazaridis-step-aside.html?_r=0.

Chapter 4

1. Charles Townes, *How the Laser Happened: Adventures of a Scientist* (Oxford: Oxford University Press, 1999).

2. Courtney Macavinta, "Recording Industry Sues Music Start-up, Cites Black Market," *CNet*, December 7, 1999, accessed July 5, 2015, http://news.cnet .com/Recording-industry-sues-music-start-up,-cites-black-market/2100-1023 _3-234092.html.

3. Of course, physical music retailers were displaced. Chains like Tower Records had no place in the new online value chain in music distribution. As was the case with Blockbuster, such chains might technically have transitioned to the new online distribution, but none of their existing assets or capabilities were of value there.

4. "About Us," *Udacity*, accessed July 5, 2015, https://www.udacity.com/us.

5. Tamar Lewin, "Instruction for Masses Knocks Down Campus Walls," *New York Times*, March 4, 2012, accessed July 5, 2015, http://www.nytimes.com/ 2012/03/05/education/moocs-large-courses-open-to-all-topple-campus-walls .html.

6. William Baumol, "Children of the Performing Arts, the Economic Dilemma: The Climbing Costs of Health Care and Education," *Journal of Cultural Economics* 20 (1996): 183–206.

7. "Average Rates of Growth of Published Charges by Decade," CollegeBoard, accessed July 5, 2015, http://trends.collegeboard.org/college-pricing/figures -tables/average-rates-growth-published-charges-decade.

8. Michael Cusumano, "Are the Costs of 'Free' Too High in Online Education?," *MIT Sloan Management Review* 56, no. 4 (2013): 1–4, accessed July 5, 2015, http://mitsloan.mit.edu/shared/ods/documents/High-Costs-of -Free-Online-Education.pdf&PubID=5082.

9. The reason was that only about 5 percent of those enrolling were achieving appropriate learning outcomes. Most dropped out, but some did not make the cut. Max Chafkin, "Udacity's Sebastian Thrun, Godfather of Free Online Education, Changes Course," *Fast Company*, December 2013/January 2014, online version accessed July 5, 2015, http://www.fastcompany.com/3021473/ udacity-sebastian-thrun-uphill-climb.

10. Maria Konnikova, "Will MOOCs Be Flukes?," *New Yorker*, November 7, 2014, accessed July 5, 2015, http://www.newyorker.com/science/maria -konnikova/moocs-failure-solutions.

11. Low achievement rates have plagued all nontraditional models. Even the for-profit University of Phoenix only graduates 17 percent of its online students. Chafkin, "Udacity's Sebastian Thrun."

12. Clay Shirky, "Napster, Udacity and the Academy," *The Clay Shirky Blog*, November 2, 2012, reposted at Case Western University, accessed July 5, 2015, http://www.case.edu/strategicplan/downloads/Napster-Udacity-and-the -Academy-Clay_Shirky.pdf.

13. Thomas Friedman, "The Professor's Big Stage," *New York Times*, March 5, 2013, accessed July 5, 2015, http://www.nytimes.com/2013/03/06/opinion/ friedman-the-professors-big-stage.html.

14. "Innovators Accelerator," accessed July 5, 2015, https://innovatorsaccelerator.com.

15. "C.G.P. Grey Channel," *YouTube* channel, accessed July 5, 2015, https://www.youtube.com/user/CGPGrey.

16. Claudia Deutsch, "Deep in Debt since 1988, Polaroid Files for Bankruptcy," *New York Times*, October 13, 2001, accessed July 5, 2015, http://www.nytimes.com/2001/10/13/business/deep-in-debt-since-1988-polaroid -files-for-bankruptcy.html. Michael Merced, "Eastman Kodak Files for Bankruptcy," *New York Times*, January 19, 2012, accessed July 5, 2015, http://dealbook.nytimes.com/2012/01/19/eastman-kodak-files-for-bankruptcy.

17. Mary Tripsas and Giovanni Gavetti, "Capabilities, Cognition, and Inertia: Evidence from Digital Imaging," *Strategic Management Journal* 21, no. 10/11 (2000): 1147–1161.

18. Ibid., 1155.

19. James Estrin, "Kodak's First Digital Moment," *New York Times*, August 12, 2015, http://lens.blogs.nytimes.com/2015/08/12/kodaks-first-digital -moment/. Kodak management were unimpressed with the digital camera prototype built by their engineer, Steven Sasson, as they couldn't envisage anyone looking at pictures on a television set rather than in print.

20. "Mistakes Made on the Road to Innovation," *Bloomberg Business*, November 26, 2006, accessed July 5, 2015, http://www.bloomberg.com/bw/ stories/2006-11-26/mistakes-made-on-the-road-to-innovation.

21. This was the article in 1999 that propelled Christensen to notoriety. Toni Mack, "Danger: Stealth Attack," *Forbes*, January 25, 1999, accessed July 5, 2015, http://www.forbes.com/forbes/1999/0125/6302088a.html?_ga=1.118239 689.1171993501.1412879415.

22. Jordan Weissmann, "What Killed Kodak?," *Atlantic*, January 5, 2012, accessed July 5, 2015, http://www.theatlantic.com/business/archive/2012/01/ what-killed-kodak/250925.

23. Brian Wu, Zhixi Wan, and Daniel Levinthal, "Complementary Assets as Pipes and Prisms: Innovation Incentives and Trajectory Choices," *Strategic Management Journal* 35, no. 9 (2013): 1257–1278.

24. Laura Montini, "How Uber and Lyft Became the Taxi Industry's Worst Nightmare," *Inc*, June 26, 2015, accessed July 5, 2015, http://www.inc.com/ laura-montini/infographic/how-uber-and-lyft-became-the-taxi-industrys-worst -nightmare.html.

25. John Hendel, "Celebrating Linotype, 125 Years since Its Debut," *Atlantic*, May 20, 2011, accessed July 5, 2015, http://www.theatlantic.com/ technology/archive/2011/05/celebrating-linotype-125-years-since-its-debut/ 238968.

26. David Teece, "Profiting from Technological Innovation: Implications for Integration, Collaboration, Licensing and Public Policy," *Research Policy* 15, no. 6 (1986): 285–305.

27. "History," *Linotype*, accessed July 5, 2015, http://www.linotype.com/49/history.html.

28. Matt McFarland, "The Unstoppable TI-84 Plus: How an Outdated Calculator Still Holds a Monopoly on Classrooms," *Washington Post*, September 2, 2014, accessed July 5, 2015, http://www.washingtonpost.com/blogs/innovations/wp/2014/09/02/the-unstoppable-ti-84-plus-how-an-outdated-calculator-still-holds-a-monopoly-on-classrooms.

Chapter 5

1. For a longer discussion of this see Joshua Gans, *Information Wants to Be Shared* (Boston: Harvard Business Review, 2012).

2. Justin Fox, "The Real Secret to Thriving amid Disruptive Innovation," *Harvard Business Review*, January 24, 2011, accessed July 5, 2015, http://blogs.hbr.org/2011/01/this-wave-of-disruptive-innova.

3. The full report was accessed from the following article: Jason Abbruzzese, "The Full New York Times Innovation Report," *Mashable*, May 16, 2014, accessed July 5, 2015, http://mashable.com/2014/05/16/full-new-york-times-innovation-report.

4. Ibid.

5. This was not implicit but explicit. They examined Kodak as a case and said "let's not end up like them."

6. Abbruzzese, "The Full New York Times Innovation Report."

7. Kenneth J. Arrow, "Economic Welfare and the Allocation of Resources for Inventions," in *The Rate and Direction of Inventive Activity*, ed. R. Nelson (Princeton: Princeton University Press, 1962).

8. Michael L. Tushman and Philip Anderson, "Technological Discontinuities and Organizational Environments," *Administrative Science Quarterly* 31 (1986): 439–465.

9. See, for example, Carl Shapiro, "Competition and Innovation: Did Arrow Hit the Bull's Eye?," in *The Rate and Direction of Inventive Activity Revisited*, ed. Josh Lerner and Scott Stern (Cambridge, MA: National Bureau of Economic Research, 2013).

10. T. Holmes, D. Levine, and J. Schmitz, "Monopoly and the Incentive to Innovate When Adoption Involves Switchover Disruptions," *American Economic Journal: Microeconomics* 4 (2012): 1–33.

11. Fred Vogelstein, "The Untold Story: How the iPhone Blew Up the Wireless Industry," *Wired*, January 9, 2008, http://archive.wired.com/gadgets/wireless/magazine/16-02/ff_iphone?currentPage=all.

12. "Verizon Wireless Announces the Next Evolution in Global Connectivity: The BlackBerry 8830 World Edition Smartphone and Global BlackBerry Service," Verizon, April 24, 2007, accessed July 5, 2015, http://www.verizonwireless.com/news/article/2007/04/pr2007-04-25.html.

13. Jacquie McNish and Sean Silcoff, *Losing the Signal: The Untold Story behind the Extraordinary Rise and Spectacular Fall of BlackBerry* (New York: HarperCollins, 2015), 140.

14. Amol Sharma and Sara Silver, "BlackBerry Storm Is Off to Bit of a Bumpy Start," *Wall Street Journal*, January 26, 2009, accessed July 5, 2015, http://www.wsj.com/articles/SB123292905716613927.

15. McNish and Silcoff, *Losing the Signal*, 140.

16. David Pogue, "No Keyboard? And You Call This a Blackberry?," *New York Times*, November 28, 2008, accessed July 5, 2015, http://www.nytimes .com/2008/11/27/technology/personaltech/27pogue.html?_r=3&em =&pagewanted=all.

17. McNish and Silcoff, *Losing the Signal*, 166.

18. Richard Gilbert and David M. G. Newbery, "Preemptive Patenting and the Persistence of Monopoly," *American Economic Review* 72, no. 3 (1981): 514–526.

19. Strictly speaking, an entrant may hope to receive "Competitive Profits" if its entry is successful, while the established firm, if its defense is successful, gets "Monopoly Profits" rather than "Competitive Profits." Thus, the established firm's investment is driven by the difference ("Monopoly Profits" − "Competitive Profits") which is greater than "Competitive Profits" if "Monopoly Profits" > 2 × "Competitive Profits," something that usually is the case.

20. A similar notion is put forward in a managerial context by Richard Foster and Sarah Kaplan, *Creative Destruction* (New York: Crown Business, 2001). There they demonstrate that when the chips are down, established firms that can attack before and over the steep portion of technology S curves can end up prevailing and perhaps retaining market leadership.

21. Cyrus Farivar and Andrew Cunningham, "The Rise and Fall of AMD: How an Underdog Stuck It to Intel," *Ars Technica*, April 21, 2013, accessed July 5, 2015, http://arstechnica.com/business/2013/04/the-rise-and-fall-of-amd -how-an-underdog-stuck-it-to-intel.

22. Michael A. Cusumano and David B. Yoffie, *Competing on Internet Time: Lessons from Netscape and Its Battle with Microsoft* (New York: Free Press, 2000).

23. Bill Gates, "The Internet Tidal Wave," Microsoft internal memo, May 26, 1995, accessed July 5, 2015, http://www.justice.gov/atr/cases/exhibits/20.pdf.

24. Constantinos Markides and Paul Geroski documented many instances where waiting and seeing was an effective and indeed desirable response for established firms. See Markides and Geroski, *Fast Second: How Smart Companies Bypass Radical Innovation to Dominate New Markets* (New York: Jossey-Bass, 2004).

25. Matt Marx, Joshua S. Gans, and David Hsu, "Dynamic Commercialization Strategies for Disruptive Technologies: Evidence from the Speech Recognition Industry," *Management Science* 60, no. 12 (2014): 3103–3123.

26. In particular, many companies asserted certain percentage claims on accuracy which could only be evaluated over time. What was most interesting from our perspective was that technologies could be classified relatively easily as disruptive or sustaining according to the demand-side theory of disruption. One example of disruptive innovation was the move from speech recognition embedded in specialized chips or hardware units to speech recognition systems that were software only. The latter initially performed worse on traditional metrics such as vocabulary size and accuracy but involved benefits in terms of cost and convenience. We found that the best of these technologies improved over time on traditional metrics and thus, at least after the fact, could be seen to be disruptive. Like disk drives, there were a few other examples of such technology innovations and a large number of sustaining innovations.

27. "Vlingo," Vlingo, accessed July 5, 2015, http://www.vlingo.com.

28. "AT&T and Vlingo to Bring Innovative Speech Recognition to Mobile Devices Worldwide," Vlingo, September 16, 2009, accessed July 5, 2015, http://blog.vlingo.com/license-att-watson.

29. By contrast, there was no difference between disruptive and sustaining entrants when it came to switching the other way (from cooperate to compete), although this was a rarer event overall.

30. David Pogue, "The Tragic Death of the Flip," *New York Times*, April 14, 2011, accessed July 5, 2015, http://pogue.blogs.nytimes.com/2011/04/14/the-tragic-death-of-the-flip.

31. Sam Grobart and Elevyn Rusli, "For Flip Camera, Four Years from Hot Start-up to Obsolete," *New York Times*, April 12, 2011, accessed July 5, 2015, http://www.nytimes.com/2011/04/13/technology/13flip.html.

32. On a final note, some have suggested that Cisco should have just unloaded Flip rather than shut it down. One suspects that it may not have been able to realize much value from that strategy for the very same reason that it could not justify future investments in Flip. But there may have been another concern. Cisco has a reputation for fair dealing in acquiring companies. Flip's owners were beneficiaries of that. But if you want a reputation for fair dealing as a buyer of a company, do you really want to unload an asset for a price higher than you think it is worth? If you don't want to be seen as a shark as a buyer, perhaps you have to forgo being a shark as a seller too.

Chapter 6

1. Brad Stone, "With Its Tablet, Apple Blurs Line between Devices," *New York Times*, January 27, 2010, accessed July 5, 2015, http://www.nytimes.com/2010/01/28/technology/companies/28apple.html?gwh=3679863732D18BB2BF3E9BA662474730&gwt=pay.

2. For an excellent account, look at Jerry Kaplan, *Startup: A Silicon Valley Adventure* (New York: Penguin Books, 1994).

3. Five years later, the iPad is a huge success and has consigned a personal computer category—the small, lightweight Netbook—to history. But otherwise it has not replaced personal computers and, indeed, Apple's own computer sales have continually outgrown the rest of the personal computer market.

4. Joe Castaldo, "How Management Has Failed at RIM," *Canadian Business*, January 19, 2012, accessed July 5, 2015, http://www.canadianbusiness.com/ technology-news/how-management-has-failed-at-rim.

5. Lazaridis quoted in Jacquie McNish and Sean Silcoff, *Losing the Signal: The Untold Story behind the Extraordinary Rise and Spectacular Fall of BlackBerry* (New York: HarperCollins, 2015), 196.

6. However, it did not strictly conform to the playbook suggested by Clayton Christensen, who argued that self-disruption needs to come before a competitor's new product and not after it, as RIM was doing.

7. Ina Fried, "Microsoft Buys Speech Recognition Company Tellme," *CNet*, March 14, 2007, accessed July 5, 2015, http://news.cnet.com/Microsoft-buys -speech-recognition-company-Tellme/2100-1001_3-6167000.html.

8. Clayton M. Christensen and Michael Raynor, *The Innovator's Solution* (Boston: Harvard Business School Press, 2003), Loc 3533.

9. Ibid.

10. Claire C. Miller and Nick Bilton, "Google's Lab of Wildest Dreams," *New York Times*, November 13, 2011, accessed July 5, 2015, http://www .nytimes.com/2011/11/14/technology/at-google-x-a-top-secret-lab-dreaming-up -the-future.html.

11. Fourth among US manufacturers with 7 percent of the market at its peak.

12. Christensen refers to them separately as Quantum-1 and Quantum-2. Clayton Christensen, "The Rigid Disk Drive Industry, 1956–90: A History of Commercial and Technological Turbulence," *Business History Review* 67 (1993): 531–588

13. "Skunkworks," Lockheed Martin, accessed July 5, 2015, http://www .lockheedmartin.com/us/aeronautics/skunkworks.html.

14. Clayton M. Christensen, *The Innovator's Dilemma* (New York: Harper Business, 2011), chapter 8.

15. Joab Jackson, "The Mainframe Turns 50, or, Why the IBM System/360 Launch Was the Dawn of Enterprise IT," *PC World*, April 7, 2014, accessed July 5, 2015, http://www.pcworld.com/article/2140220/the-mainframe-turns -50-or-why-the-ibm-system360-launch-was-the-dawn-of-enterprise-it.html.

16. Timothy Bresnahan, Shane Greenstein, and Rebecca Henderson, "Schumpeterian Economies and Diseconomies of Scope: Illustrations from the Histories of IBM and Microsoft," in *The Rate and Direction of Inventive Activity Revisited*, ed. Josh Lerner and Scott Stern (Chicago: University of Chicago Press, 2012), 217.

17. For a full account, see Bill Lowe and Cary Sherburne, *No-Nonsense Innovation* (New York: Morgan James, 2009).

18. In a series of influential papers on the automobile assembly industry, Sharon Novak and Scott Stern uncovered important patterns in vertical integration versus outsourcing. First, they found that firms developed capabilities for integration or else for outsourcing so much that they tended to be predominantly of one form or the other. Second, they found that firms that outsourced auto components tended to have higher-quality products in early model years (as measured by *Consumer Reports* ratings) but that the trajectory of improvement in those products over model years was inferior to that of their vertically integrated counterparts. Together this suggests that there are strong forces pushing firms to be integrated or not, rather than some hybrid. Sharon Novak and Scott Stern, "Complementarity among Vertical Integration Decisions: Evidence from Automobile Product Development," *Management Science 55*, no. 2 (2009): 311–332.

19. Bresnahan, Greenstein, and Henderson, "Schumpeterian Economies and Diseconomies of Scope," 227.

20. "Send in the Clones," Computer History Museum, accessed July 5, 2015, http://www.computerhistory.org/revolution/personal-computers/17/302.

21. Bresnahan, Greenstein, and Henderson, "Schumpeterian Economies and Diseconomies of Scope," 232–233.

22. Ibid., 239.

23. Robert A. Burgelman, "Fading Memories: A Process Theory of Strategic Business Exit in Dynamic Environments," *Administrative Science Quarterly 39*, no. 1 (1994): 24.

24. Ibid.

25. Jenny Williams, "RIM Posts 33% Annual Sales Increase as It Prepares for Playbook Launch," *Computer Weekly*, March 25, 2011, accessed July 5, 2015, http://www.computerweekly.com/news/1280095527/RIM-posts-33-annual-sales -increase-as-it-prepares-for-Playbook-launch.

26. Luke Reimer, "BMM Hackathons: An International Invasion!," Blackberry, November 16, 2011, accessed July 5, 2015, http://devblog.blackberry.com/ 2011/11/bbm-hackathons-international.

27. McNish and Silcoff, *Losing the Signal*, 205.

28. Ibid., 204.

29. Sarah Frier, "Facebook $22 Billion Whatsapp Deal Buys $10 Million in Sales," *Bloomberg Business*, October 28, 2014, accessed July 5, 2015, http://www.bloomberg.com/news/articles/2014-10-28/facebook-s-22-billion -whatsapp-deal-buys-10-million-in-sales.

30. McNish and Silcoff, *Losing the Signal*, 224.

31. Ibid., 232.

32. "Research in Motion to Acquire QNX Software Systems from Harman International," QNX, accessed July 5, 2015, http://www.qnx.com/news/pr _4114_1.html.

33. Will Connors and Chip Cummins, "RIM Takes Playbook Hit," December 3, 2011, accessed July 5, 2015, http://www.wsj.com/articles/SB10001424052970204012004577073932113176106.

Chapter 7

1. Rebecca Henderson, "Underinvestment and Incompetence as Responses to Radical Innovation: Evidence from the Photolithographic Alignment Equipment Industry," *RAND Journal of Economics* 24, no. 2 (1993): 248–270.

2. Rebecca Henderson and Kim B. Clark, "Architectural Innovation: The Reconfiguration of Existing Product Technologies and the Failure of Established Firms," *Administrative Science Quarterly* 35, no. 1 (1990): 9–30.

3. Ibid.

4. Ibid., 261.

5. That is, proximity printers, scanning projection aligners, and step-and-repeat aligners.

6. Rebecca Henderson, "Breaking the Chains of Embedded Knowledge: Architectural Innovation as a Source of Competitive Advantage," *Design Management Journal* 2, no. 3 (1991): 43–47.

7. Rebecca Henderson, "Product Development Capability as a Strategic Weapon: Canon's Experience in the Photolithographic Alignment Equipment Industry," in *Managing Product Development*, ed. Toshiro Hitotsubashi (Oxford: Oxford University Press, 1996), 272.

8. Ibid.

9. In her book *The Silo Effect* (New York: Simon and Schuster, 2015), Gillian Tett describes the procedures by which Facebook inducts new engineers into its company. Those engineers enter as a cohort and receive the same induction (over many weeks) regardless of where they end up. That way, there is a cross-pollination of social interactions across divisions that may last as long as a person's career. The purpose of this is to break down silos that might form and impede the firm's ability to adjust to new innovations in the future.

10. There is a large literature on such capabilities in strategic management. The most significant part involves the notion of dynamic capabilities, which are capabilities that allow firms to flexibly deal with large events—such as disruptive and architectural innovations—although the scope is more than just that. See David Teece, Gary Pisano, and Amy Shuen, "Dynamic Capabilities and Strategic Management," *Strategic Management Journal* 18, no. 7 (1997): 509–533.

11. "The Last Kodak Moment?," *Economist*, January 4, 2012, accessed July 5, 2015, http://www.economist.com/node/21542796.

12. Mary Tripsas, "Exploring the Interaction between Organizational Identity and Organization Architecture in Technological Transitions," mimeo, Harvard Business School (2011).

13. Ibid., 10.

14. Part of this study is published as Janet Vertesi and Paul Dourish, "The Value of Data: Considering the Context of Production in Data Economies," in *Proceedings of the 2011 ACM Conference on Computer Supported Cooperative Work (CSCW 2011)* (New York: Association for Computing Machinery, 2011), 533–542. Other insight is contained in Janet Vertesi, *Seeing Like a Rover: How Robots, Teams, and Images Craft Knowledge of Mars* (Chicago: University of Chicago Press, 2015).

15. Why? Because Vertesi is still working with them and prefers to keep them somewhat disguised. She has written a book on the Mars Rover missions, so you can get a clue there, but in one of the papers that her talk was based on she hides the mission locations (Vertesi, *Seeing Like a Rover*).

16. "Monotype Imaging Acquires Linotype," Linotype, August 2, 2006, accessed July 5, 2015, http://www.linotype.com/de/2794/ monotypeimagingacquireslinotype.html.

17. "Monotype Acquires Swyft Media," Monotype, February 2, 2015, accessed July 5, 2015, http://ir.monotype.com/investor-relations/press-releases/press -release-details/2015/Monotype-Acquires-Swyft-Media/default.aspx.

Chapter 8

1. Perhaps the most famous of these studies is an article by Jill Lepore, "The Disruption Machine," *New Yorker*, June 23, 2014, http://www.newyorker.com/ magazine/2014/06/23/the-disruption-machine. While that article pointed out that failures in the industry did not follow Christensen's 1997 predictions, Lepore had a broader agenda that had more to do with the widespread and unfettered use of disruption to justify managerial practices than with the hard disk drive industry itself. Lepore certainly did not consider the broader academic literature, as I do here.

2. In *The Innovator's Dilemma*, Christensen examined the steel, excavation, and discount retailing markets and found that they supported his demand-side theory of disruption. (Clayton Christensen, *The Innovator's Dilemma* [Boston: Harvard Business School Press, 1997].) I am not going to examine these here as, in each case, there was a single disruptive innovation identified, making it hard to evaluate the evidence without in-depth knowledge of each industry. Some of these stories have been controversial (see, for example, Erwin Daneels, "Disruptive Technology Reconsidered: A Critique and Research Agenda," *Journal of Product Innovation Management* 21, no. 4 [2004]: 246–258; Lepore, "The Disruption Machine"). For instance, Christensen argues that mini-mills were able to compete for the low-end part of the steel industry (notably, rebar) away from the larger integrated steel mills. That is certainly true, but it was unclear whether the response from established firms was due to disruption or other reasons (e.g., unionization). Moreover, since Christensen's work, the advance of mini-mills appears to have been halted,

with the largest steel producers in the world being integrated; even within the US, US Steel, for example, produces as much steel as mini-mill leader Nucor, and both have recently entered into alliances moving them closer to integration.

3. Christensen himself has advertised to his students and others that he is always looking for anomalies, as they help him challenge his own theories. See Anne Bosman, "Anomalies Wanted: Challenging the Theory of Disruptive Innovation," *HBX Blog*, July 7, 2015 (http://www.hbxblog.com/anomalies -wanted-challenging-the-theory-of-disruptive-innovation).

4. Clayton Christensen, "The Rigid Disk Drive Industry, 1956–90: A History of Commercial and Technological Turbulence," *Business History Review* 67 (1993): 531–588, considers innovations up to 1989; he chooses not to classify the 14-inch and 2.5-inch step changes as disruptive innovations. Interestingly, he argues that each of them not only involved a "shrinking [of] the size of the components used," but that "each involved significant redesign of the way components interacted within the architecture" (549). He argues that the 14-inch and 2.5-inch drives were introduced by established firms (as table 8.1 depicts), and so he classifies them as sustaining. To my mind, given that these drives did, in fact, reduce performance (in terms of capacity) for the mainstream customers at the time, it is not appropriate to classify them in that way; hence my choice to include them in table 8.1. Christensen, however, argues that customers, for instance, of 3.5-inch drives led established firms "across the architectural transition" (568). That is, the leading laptop makers—Toshiba, Sharp, and Zenith—also became the leading notebook manufacturers and so valued a similar set of performance attributes "such as ruggedness, low power consumption, and capacity per unit of weight and volume" (569). So while 2.5-inch drives were not sustaining according to the metric Christensen used to classify technologies previously, he claimed that they were sustaining according to a broader or evolved metric of performance. When 1.8-inch drives were introduced, he argued that the existing classification technique could be reapplied. (See Christensen, *The Innovator's Dilemma*.) All this is to, say, as I noted earlier in the book, that it is sometimes a challenge to consider the performance metric from the position of an outside observer in the industry that drives customer preferences at the time.

5. John Markoff, "Control Data to Sell Unit to Seagate," *New York Times*, June 3, 1989, accessed July 5, 2015, http://www.nytimes.com/1989/06/13/ business/control-data-to-sell-unit-to-seagate.html.

6. John Markoff, "Alan F. Shugart, 76, a Developer of Disk Drive Industry, Dies," *New York Times,* December 15, 2006, accessed July 5, 2015, http:// www.nytimes.com/2006/12/15/obituaries/15shugart.html?_r=3&oref=slogin&.

7. James Bates, "Firm's Loss of Executive Dims Future: Conner's Exit Seen as Serious Blow to Computer Memories," *Los Angeles Times*, October 15, 1985, accessed July 5, 2015, http://articles.latimes.com/1985-10-15/business/ fi-16428_1_finis-conner.

8. "Company News; Tandon Sells Disk Drive Unit," *New York Times*, March 9, 1998, accessed July 5, 2015, http://www.nytimes.com/1988/03/09/business/company-news-tandon-sells-disk-drive-unit.html.

9. "WD Acquires Hitachi GST," Western Digital, accessed July 5, 2015, http://www.wdc.com/en/company/hgst.

10. David McKendrick, Richard Doner, and Stephan Haggard, *From Silicon Valley to Singapore: Location and Competitive Advantage in the Hard Disk Drive Industry* (Palo Alto, CA: Stanford Business Books, 2000).

11. Tim Bresnahan and Shane Greenstein, "Technological Competition and the Structure of the Computer Industry," *Journal of Industrial Economics* 47, no. 1 (2003): 1–40.

12. It is worth noting that the notion that each drive size appealed to a different class of computer manufacturers is controversial. Christensen concluded that while 14-inch manufacturers targeted mainframes, 8-inch went to minicomputers, 5.25-inch to personal computers, 3.5-inch to portable computers, 1.8-inch to heart-monitoring devices, and 1.3-inch to personal digital assistants. By contrast, McKendrick and his coauthors noted that minicomputer firms used 14-inch disks for many years before 8-inch ones were made, including one supplied by Control Data—the leading maker of mainframe storage. That firm was the first to make a push to serve minicomputer makers, five years before the first 8-inch drive was introduced. The same was true for other incumbents such as IBM, Century Data, and Digital Equipment which actually led the minicomputer manufacturing market. McKendrick, Doner, and Haggard, *From Silicon Valley to Singapore*.

13. Similarly for the 3.5-inch market, which Christensen argued was targeted at portable computer manufacturers. Rodime, a disk drive manufacturer that had produced a 5.25-inch model, was actually the first firm to ship a 3.5-inch model. In fact, Rodime was initially selling 3.5-inch models in a 5.25 chassis and also counted Apple—at that time only making desktops—as one of its large customers. Significant traction for the market, however, did not occur until three years later when Conner Peripherals signed a deal with one of its key investors, Compaq Computers, signaling support for Conner's entry into 3.5-inch drives (in order to bolster its own plans for portable computers). Consequently, these events do not fit into the notion that entrants are the only firms that successfully target new customer segments.

14. April M. Franco and Darren Filson, "Spin-outs: Knowledge Diffusion through Employee Mobility," *RAND Journal of Economics* 37, no. 4 (2006): 841–860. Their findings are confirmed by an international study by Hank W. Chesbrough, "The Organizational Impact of Technological Change: A Comparative Theory of National Institutional Factors," *Industrial and Corporate Change* 8, no. 3 (1999): 447–485. Importantly, Franco and Filson examined the hard disk drive industry systematically and found that employee mobility from incumbents to entrants of a particular type they term "spin-outs" was correlated with future success in the industry. Moreover, as will be

discussed in detail below, Andrew King and Chris Tucci, who studied this industry over the same period as Christensen, showed in 2002 that the experience of personnel drove firm success. Andrew A. King and Christopher L. Tucci, "Incumbent Entry into New Market Niches: The Role of Experience and Managerial Choice in the Creation of Dynamic Capabilities," *Management Science* 48, no. 2 (2002): 171–186.

15. Mitsuru Igami, "Estimating the Innovator's Dilemma: Structural Analysis of Creative Destruction in the Hard Disk Drive Industry," *Journal of Political Economy* (forthcoming, 2015).

16. James Porter, *Disk/Trend Report: Rigid Disk Drives*, annual (Mountain View, CA: Disk/Trend, 1978–1999).

17. Josh Lerner, "An Empirical Exploration of a Technology Race," *RAND Journal of Economics* 28, no. 2 (1997): 228.

18. Writing from his position in 1992, Christensen argued that Conner would overtake Seagate. In fact, by 1988 Seagate had already made a comeback. Lawrence M. Fisher, "Seagate Agrees to Buy Conner Peripherals," *New York Times*, September 21, 1995, accessed July 5, 2015, http://www.nytimes.com/1995/09/21/business/seagate-agrees-to-buy-conner-peripherals.html.

19. Ibid.

20. Recent research suggests that in the hard disk industry, while consolidation has been persistent and in recent times has been the dominant pattern of exit for entrants, its impact on innovation is harder to parse. See Mitsuru Igami and Kosuke Uetake, "Mergers, Innovation and Entry-Exit Dynamics: The Consolidation of the Hard Disk Drive Industry," mimeo, Yale University, July 2, 2015.

21. Eric Bangeman, "Seagate Acquires Maxtor," *ArsTechnica*, December 21, 2005, accessed July 5, 2015, http://arstechnica.com/uncategorized/2005/12/5816-2.

22. Mark Hachman, "Seagate Buys Samsung's Hard-Drive Biz for $1.375B," *PCMag*, April 11, 2011, accessed July 5, 2015, http://www.pcmag.com/article2/0,2817,2383812,00.asp.

23. Terrence O'Brien, "Seagate Completes Purchase of LaCie in Quest to Become King of the Hard Drive Hill," *Engadget*, August 3, 2012, accessed July 5, 2015, http://www.engadget.com/2012/08/03/seagate-completes-purchase-lacie.

24. "Company News; Maxtor Acquires Miniscribe Assets," *New York Times*, July 3, 1990, accessed July 5, 2015, http://www.nytimes.com/1990/07/03/business/company-news-maxtor-acquires-miniscribe-assets.html.

25. Joe Wilcox, "Maxtor Buys Rival Quantum to Become Biggest Drive Maker," *CNet*, October 4, 2000, accessed July 5, 2015, http://news.cnet.com/Maxtor-buys-rival-Quantum-to-become-biggest-drive-maker/2100-1001_3-246572.html.

26. King and Tucci, "Incumbent Entry into New Market Niches."

27. Christensen was critical of King and Tucci's study because they looked at all of the innovations in the hard disk industry rather than sort and eliminate them as Christensen had done. See Clayton Christensen, "The Ongoing Process of Building a Theory of Disruption," *Journal of Product Innovation Management* 23 (2006): 39–55. King and Tucci's approach is the accepted means of testing theories and allows them to eliminate bias in data selection.

28. Andrew King and Christopher Tucci, "Can Old Disk Drive Companies Learn New Tricks?," mimeo (2002), Tuck School of Management, Dartmouth College.

29. McKendrick, Doner, and Haggard, *From Silicon Valley to Singapore*, Loc 3640.

30. Ibid., Loc 119.

31. In recent research, Mitsuru Igami has found that hard disk drive makers that maintained offshore component production and assembly tended to have higher survival rates in the industry. See Igami, "Offshoring under Oligopoly," BFI Working Paper Series, no. 2015-04, April 2015.

32. Clayton Christensen, Fernando Suárez, and Jim Utterback, "Strategies for Survival in Fast-Changing Industries," *Management Science* 44 (1998): 207–220. Interestingly, the paper does not mention disruptive innovation or disruption at all.

33. Of course, the industry continues to evolve. Flash storage was noted by Christensen as a large and potentially disruptive technology back in 1997, and since then broader solid-state storage has become a staple for mobile devices and, more recently, laptops. Will this overturn the market leadership of the three remaining hard disk drive manufacturers? It is hard to speculate, but in late 2015 Western Digital offered to pay $19 billion for the leading flash drive maker, SanDisk. So if flash is a disruptive technology, Western Digital has managed this by acquisition. Chad Bray, "Western Digital to Buy Memory Chip Maker SanDisk for $19 Billion," *New York Times*, October 21, 2015, http://www.nytimes.com/2015/10/22/business/dealbook/western-digital-to-buy-memory-chip-maker-sandisk-for-19-billion.html?_r=0.

Chapter 9

1. That is, Episode IV, *A New Hope*.

2. "Apple Death Knell Counter," last modified May 4, 2015, http://www.macobserver.com/tmo/death_knell.

3. Peter Burrows, "How Apple Could Mess Up, Again," *Bloomberg Business*, January 9, 2006, accessed July 5, 2015, http://www.businessweek.com/stories/2006-01-09/how-apple-could-mess-up-againbusinessweek-business-news-stock-market-and-financial-advice.

4. Ben Thompson, "What Clayton Christensen Got Wrong," *Stratechery*, September 22, 2014, accessed July 5, 2015, http://stratechery.com/2013/clayton-christensen-got-wrong/.

5. "Apple to Acquire Beats Music & Beats Electronics," last modified May 28, 2014, https://www.apple.com/pr/library/2014/05/28Apple-to-Acquire-Beats-Music-Beats-Electronics.html.

6. Jena McGregor, "Clayton Christensen's Innovation Brain," *Bloomberg Business*, June 15, 2007, accessed July 5, 2015, http://www.businessweek.com/stories/2007-06-15/clayton-christensens-innovation-brainbusinessweek-business-news-stock-market-and-financial-advice.

7. Anders Brownworth and Horace Dediu, "An Interview with Clayton Christensen," podcast 36, *The Critical Path*, MP3, May 2, 2012, accessed July 5, 2015, http://5by5.tv/criticalpath/36.

8. Christensen as transcribed by Forbes. Steve Denning, "Why Clayton Christensen Worries about Apple," *Forbes*, May 7, 2012, accessed July 5, 2015, http://www.forbes.com/sites/stevedenning/2012/05/07/why-clayton-christensen-worries-about-apple.

9. We have snippets from various accounts that suggest how Apple achieved integration across all of these divisions. In *Becoming Steve Jobs*, Brent Schlender and Rick Tetzeli describe how Jobs would spend his day moving between various product design teams and, like a bee spreading pollen, would seed and link the direction of those teams to one another. This would make him a heavy-handed, cross-functional product design manager who just happened to be the CEO of the company. After Jobs left in 2011, there was a gap in this function, and in short order the new CEO, Tim Cook, gave Jonny Ive control of both hardware and software design (he had previously only managed hardware). This was a recognition that Apple needed a manager who was responsible for both key aspects of the business and, in some sense, could preserve and renew architectural innovation and linkages across all of its products. Brent Schelder and Rick Tetzeli, *Becoming Steve Jobs: The Evolution of a Reckless Upstart into a Visionary Leader* (New York: Crown Business, 2015).

10. Farhad Manjoo, "A Murky Road Ahead for Android Despite Market Dominance," *New York Times*, May 27, 2015, accessed July 5, 2015, http://www.nytimes.com/2015/05/28/technology/personaltech/a-murky-road-ahead-for-android-despite-market-dominance.html?_r=0.

11. Although it may well not listen to customers because it hires people who are just like its customers. See Joshua Gans and Eric von Hippel, "To Stay Ahead of Disruption's Curve, Follow Lead Users," *Harvard Business Review*, December 17, 2012, accessed July 5, 2015, https://hbr.org/2012/12/to-stay-ahead-of-disruptions-curve.

12. Apple wanted to integrate with its mobile software without the need for cooperation with Google.

13. Jobs was worried about cloud services and told his biographer, Walter Isaacson, how important transforming to the cloud would be. Christensen was explicitly in his mind and Jobs did not want to be left behind; hence Apple was pursuing a doubling-up strategy.

Index

Abernathy, Bill, 18, 40, 139n11
Acquisitions, 76–78, 97, 123–125,
    131
Adner, Ron, 38, 142n15
Advanced Technology Group, 3, 11
Advertising revenue, for newspaper,
    65, 146n1
Air travel industry, 59
Alchian, Armin, 41, 143n21
AMD, 74
Anderson, Philip, 68, 69, 146n8
Android phones, 39, 45, 132,
    143n18, 157n10
"Anomalies," 115–116, 153n3
Apple. *See also* iPad; iPhone; iPod
    acquisition of Beats Music, 131,
    157n5
    and architectural knowledge, 133
    avoiding disruption, 133, 144,
    157n11
    doubling down, 70–72
    future prospects, 129–134, 144n5,
    156nn2–4
    map products, 133, 157n12
    vs. Nokia, 34–25
    prices of, 37, 38, 39
    theory of disruption and, 131,
    157nn7–8
Architectural innovations
    and established firms, 44–45, 143n25
    firms and dealing with, 45–46, 98,
    143n27
    Henderson and Clark on, 22–24,
    44–45, 100–101, 151nn2–4

key, 127
    and Netflix, 24
Architectural knowledge
    and Apple, 133
    Cannon innovation in, 103, 132
    employing, 104, 151n9
    and Henderson-Clark theory,
    43–45
    and incumbents, 45, 143n26
    in organizations, 43, 47, 84
    and supply-side disruption, 79
    tacit, 102, 151n6
Arrow, Kenneth, 42, 68,
    143nn23–24
AT&T, 70
Automatic speed recognition (ASR)
    industry, 77–78, 84, 147n25,
    148nn26–29, 149n7
Autonomy, to avoid dilemmas, 84, 95

Balsillie, Jim, 94
Banking industry, 60
Baumol, William, 50
BBM, 93–94, 150nn26–28, 150n30
Bell Labs, 49, 143n1
BlackBerry
    and Apple, 33, 35, 36, 38, 141n7,
    142n10
    and demand side of disruption, 41
    hardware of, 46, 71
    Messenger or BBM, 93–94,
    150nn26–28, 150n30
    reinventing, 149n5
    Storm, 71, 72, 83, 147n14, 149n4